WHO'S LAUGHING NOW? **THE STORY OF**

JESSIE J

Cover designed by Fresh Lemon
Picture research by Jacqui Black

ISBN: 978.1.78038.313.2
Order No: OP54505

Exclusive Distributors
Music Sales Limited,
14/15 Berners Street,
London, W1T 3LJ.

Music Sales Corporation,
257 Park Avenue South,
New York, NY 10010, USA.

Macmillan Distribution Services,
56 Parkwest Drive
Derrimut, Vic 3030,
Australia.

Every effort has been made to trace the copyright holders of the photographs in this book but one or two were unreachable. We would be grateful if the photographers concerned would contact us.

Printed in the EU

A catalogue record for this book is available from the British Library.

Visit Omnibus Press on the web at www.omnibuspress.com

WHO'S LAUGHING NOW? **THE STORY OF**

JESSIE J

CHLOE GOVAN

OMNIBUS PRESS
London / New York / Paris / Sydney / Copenhagen / Berlin / Madrid / Tokyo

Dedication

In memory of my much loved grandmother Maggie Armitage who suffered a stroke, like Jessie, and passed away just after the writing of this book.

Contents

Contents

v

Acknowledgements

A special thanks goes to interviewees Kerry Louise Barnaby, Natalie Green, Kelly Kim Kranstoun, Aisha Ludmilla, Myke Rayon, Shae, Dawn Wenn-Kober and all the additional anonymous names who agreed to be interviewed.

Chapter 1

The Heartache That Wouldn't Go Away

"Stomp, stomp, I've arrived!"

Jessie J

White stilettos. Criminally short mini skirts. Brutal catfights that leave bloodstains on designer handbags, ripped hair extensions strewn on the street and fearsomely long fake nails torn right off. Drunken brawls that see policemen blinking nervously and wondering whether or not to intervene. Furious girls on the warpath cutting figures more formidable than the Kray Twins. Social and sexual butterflies taking to the streets in perilously high heels and sporting tans a deeper shade of orange than an Easyjet flight to Ibiza. Gaggles of drunken girls giggling raucously before falling head first out of nightclubs and descending haplessly into pools of their own vomit. Where was the scene of the crime? The location, of course, was Essex – and the birth place of Jessie J.

Born on March 27, 1988, and christened Jessica Ellen Cornish, the singer to be could little have known the stereotypes her postcode would have in store for her. Her home borough of Redbridge was a no man's land between the insalubrious urban decay of gritty, edgy East London and the superficial, larger than life glamour of central Essex, complete

1

with its self-tanning parlours, spas, nail salons and all you can drink nightclubs.

Aside from the after hours parties and polluted, allegedly sewage-infested beaches, Essex was best known for its women, who – much to their indignation – had gained the reputation from hell. This county was home to every stereotype that Amy Winehouse had sneeringly paid tribute to on her single 'Fuck Me Pumps'. The caustic song had poked fun at girls who displayed a combination of debauchery and stupidity – an opinion of Essex girls shared by many others.

According to long-standing jokes, these girls sported bra sizes bigger than their brain sizes – and Essex girls with "half a brain" were cruelly dubbed "gifted". They weren't known for their sexual restraint either, allegedly wearing pants for no other reason than to keep their ankles warm.

Time magazine poked fun at the stereotype too, claiming: "In the typology of the British, there is a special place reserved for the Essex girl, a lady from London's eastern suburbs who dresses in white strappy sandals and sun-tan oil, streaks her hair blonde, has a command of Spanish that runs only to the word Ibiza and perfects an air of tarty prettiness."

One indignant blogger lost his rag at hearing one Essex joke too many, stepping in to defend: "I am an Essex lad and frankly all of you who are choosing to tar all Essex girls with the same brush are clueless idiots – and, by the looks of it, that's most of you!"

Ouch. Yet as much as they might protest their innocence, the die for postcode stereotyping had already been cast. The term "Essex girl" had been born when Jessie was just a year old and not yet out of nappies. It all began – just like so many other stories about Essex – with an ill-fated sexual encounter. Two girls stepped forward to the tabloids in 1989 to loudly and proudly proclaim that they'd both slept with all five members of a famous boy band on the same night. The phrase "No sex please, we're British" clearly did not apply to Essex.

An intentionally provocative accompanying photo shoot appearing alongside their tabloid confessions saw the pair wearing barely there dresses and, of course, white stilettos, which became the infamous trademark of the county. The shoes also became a trademark for debauchery – and some might say the two were one and the same.

The pair paved the way for women high on beauty but low on scruples who realised that their looks were a form of currency to be exploited and traded in for such goodies as wild sex with attractive partners, bagging a rich husband or getting their own way in various regards. It was an extension of the "Daddy's girl" persona but extended to the wider world. Some called them smart, while others branded them devoid of morals. Either way, their liberation was a bitter pill to swallow for the majority of a then civilised, orderly and respectable British society.

The eighties had been a time of sexual restraint, prompted by the arrival of AIDS in the Western world at the start of the decade. Not only was casual sex risky, but condoms were discouraged, implying that the only safe options were marriage and abstinence. While religious puritans still objected to abortion in Jessie's ancestral homeland of Ireland, back then it was forbidden altogether – and birth control was frowned upon. Women were instead expected to find a husband for life.

For example, in 1987, adverts for birth control were banned by the Independent Broadcasting Authority, who insisted these could influence young people into "thinking premarital sex was normal". Durex almost went bankrupt because mid-market tabloids such as the *Daily Mail* banned their adverts from what it considered to be a respectable "family newspaper". In one case, a photo depicting a pair of intertwined feet under bed covers alongside the phrase "I hope he's being careful" was censored lest it outrage readers' morals. In previous years, even the Yellow Pages had been forbidden from advertising products under the illicit category "Contraception".

Against a backdrop of the ultra-conservative eighties, when some women were branded sluts just for dropping their pants before their wedding day, this spelled trouble for the freedom-loving Essex girls. It was an era when men were desperate to secure chastity in their wives, one where the stereotype dividing Madonnas from whores really applied. In fact, one 1980 survey revealed that half of the supposedly liberated male respondents – all under 25 – wanted to marry virgins. "I'm not [a virgin] but I would like [my wife] to be," one explained. "I just would not like the idea of a second-hand woman."

Add a couple of brash, lascivious, shamelessly lustful, unmarried good-time girls from Essex with a penchant for orgies into the equation and the problem begins to come into focus. From that moment, the reputation that linked Essex with bimbos and sex-crazed nymphets was set in stone. As the old saying goes, credibility was like virginity – and, in both cases, it could only be lost once.

A BBC report rationalised: "Statistically Essex girls were no more sexually promiscuous, nor were they of lower intelligence, than their counterparts in any other part of the UK." However, listeners were far from convinced and the county became the subject of ridicule from then onwards.

To jokers, an Essex girl's academic knowledge barely extended past the basic sex education biology – and, judging by the scale of unwanted teenage pregnancies, some might say it didn't even extend to that. According to the stereotypes, schooling for an Essex girl consisted of how to bag a footballer and how to perfect the full-on, trashy, drag queen-inspired glamour look which was all a budding Essex woman needed to get by. People across the nation jibed that the best way to make an Essex girl laugh on a Saturday was to tell her a joke on Wednesday and that the difference between Bigfoot and an intelligent Essex girl was that there had actually been sightings of Bigfoot.

The jokes snowballed, and included a jibe that their favourite form of protection was the bus shelters in which they had sex. One gag was: "What does an Essex girl say after sex?", with the response "Do you REALLY all play for the same football team?" No doubt that taunt was inspired by the groupies of the boy band.

Meanwhile the town where Jessie grew up and spent most of her childhood was the subject of the cruellest joke of all. A girl involved in a traumatic car crash and trapped in the wreckage is asked: "Where are you bleeding from?" only to answer "Bleeding Romford!"

At the tender age of one, Jessie could not have known the history of her home town – but she was soon to find out. Just a short distance from the fake nails, fake breasts, fake hair and fake eyelashes of flamboyant central Essex was her own place of birth, Romford. While towns like Brentwood might have attracted occasional, small-scale petty thieves,

Romford – and the borough of Redbridge as a whole – was felt to be a fully fledged crime hotspot.

Local gangs terrorised residents, with Ilford's library of all places being the location of countless broad-daylight muggings. Many took place at the hands of a powerful group calling themselves the Afghan Gang. The London borough of Redbridge was placed ninth highest for car theft and was generally better known for gang violence than buoyant nightlife, with around 16,000 people each year said to have been directly affected by crime.

On one occasion during Jessie's childhood, there were five near-fatal stabbings in the area in one day. A resident nonchalantly chuckled: "There are stabbings and shootings here all the time." He advised out-of-towners who could be on a visit: "You might as well be done with it and book two weeks all inclusive in Kabul."

In fact, its reputation was so flawed that a local drama group had once made the borough the scene of their own specially adapted crime thriller, *Murder On The Leyton Orient Express*. The group hoped to portray that the truth was always darker – and stranger – than fiction. As for the local girls that lived here, they were said to have more prison-cell mug shots than Facebook photographs – and, on both counts, it was a lot.

There was a backdrop of poverty and social deprivation in the area too – although Jessie's parents both held down respectable jobs, nearly a quarter of children lived in households whose members relied exclusively on state benefits. To add to the unrest, there were growing tensions over immigration. Redbridge had become the UK's most ethnically diverse borough, with 40 per cent of residents being from a racial minority. Some suspected it wouldn't be too long before, in their little area, the minority would become the majority.

With jobs in short supply following the recession and – for many – poverty and destitution just around the corner, native Londoners were becoming resentful. While some appreciated the diversity, others perceived that immigrants were moving in on their territory and merely grumbled: "How am I going to feed my children?"

Some tried to make crime pay their way to otherwise elusive privileges, while more honest members of society found themselves constantly looking over their shoulders in anticipation of either burglary or a visit from the bailiffs. Plus, if the rumours were to be believed, Romford was more violent than wartime Kabul and had about as much monogamous morality as Tiger Woods.

Yet this was the location, deep in the hinterlands of suburban East London, where a certain pop star would begin her life – and, soon after, she would have a yearning to break away from the restraints of her postcode and seek a more exciting, liberating life on the stage.

Enter Jessie J. Naturally, someone who would go on to be a performer ought to have had a dramatic stage entrance – and she didn't disappoint. While most children's first words were generic terms such as "daddy", "dog" or "ball", Jessie, on the other hand, didn't utter a single word until the age of two. However, when she did, it was a phrase that showed an instant affinity with the world of music showbiz.

While fellow entertainer Robbie Williams had proudly proclaimed that his first word had been "fuck", Jessie had gone one step further in the outrageous stakes to prove her love of the stage. Asked when music began to have a real impact on her life, she told *Gigwise*: "My first words were 'jam hot'. My sisters used to sing: 'This is the boys from the big bad city, this is jam hot'. My mum was like, 'Momma' and I used to reply 'jam hot'." She added mischievously: "My mum was very disappointed!"

The words were part of the 1990 tune 'Dub Be Good To Me' by Beats International, a song so popular it would later be covered by Faithless and Dido, The Ting Tings and – in his own version, 'Just Be Good To Green' – Professor Green featuring Lily Allen.

Jessie was ahead of her time – "jam hot" would later go on to take its place in the urban dictionary.

However, she'd been a late developer in speech, with the typical child speaking their first words at a year old and a small minority chattering away as early as six months. Jessie started speaking a year later than the national average and it was feared that she was mildly dyslexic – but she soon caught up, using her love of song as her motivation.

"It just goes to show that everyone has their niche," an anonymous friend of Jessie's told the author. "Everyone has something they're good at, even if it's not the conventional stuff like maths and English, or the normal way of measuring intelligence. Everyone has a talent, something that can inspire them to do what they thought they never could – they just have to find it."

Jessie's first experience of finding that talent was being thrust into the limelight unexpectedly on a family holiday, lisping away to nursery rhymes onstage while her proud parents looked on, camcorder in hand. "My first musical performance memory was my sister playing 'Twinkle Twinkle Little Star' on the recorder," she recalled to *I Like Music*. "I was three and I was singing. It was at a caravan park and it was an open audition for anyone on holiday. I just totally forgot the words and started laughing!"

She added to Neon Limelight: "That was my first little taste of [fame]. I was really young and it was really awful. I was just standing there and I started humming and singing out of tune."

What was more, her parents had no intention of sparing her blushes – they filmed the whole event and played it back to her throughout her childhood. For Jessie, it was eye-wateringly embarrassing, but that was no deterrent for her sisters Hannah and Rachel – five and seven years old respectively – who took every opportunity to tease her about it.

Not to be outdone, Jessie got her own back by practising – and the family was soon subjected to a three-year-old, an eight-year-old and a ten-year-old all singing their hearts out in the front room. They formed a group called The Three Cornish Pasties – a pun on their surname – and put on a show for anyone who would listen.

"Me and my sisters were in a fake girl group," Jessie told *Global Grind* with a touch of sarcasm. "We used to do shows for our aunts and uncles on a Saturday afternoon and that kind of tied in with my love of performing. My sister would play trombone and my other sister would play piano and I would have to sing a song like *Aladdin* or something irritating."

Even then, Jessie had been subversive, finding traditional song and dance routines "annoying" and wanting to experiment. She didn't have to wait long. Her mother, a former ballet dancer turned nursery school teacher, was keen for Jessie to learn the ropes and follow in her footsteps.

Living up to the precocious stage-child stereotype, Jessie trained at dance school every weekend from the age of four. "Me and my sisters would go to ballet on a Saturday morning, then it became something I was obsessed with – tap, modern and jazz dancing, then singing and acting as well," she told *This Is Essex*.

Yet how would her cash-strapped parents afford the fees? Although Jessie had never been poor, she wasn't the archetypal wealthy stage-school kid with millionaire parents and a detached mansion in the country. Living so close to central London had taken its toll on the family finances – growing up, a bowling trip to Dundee or a break in Cornwall was the closest Jessie would ever get to an exotic holiday. Instead, mundane caravan parks in middle England were the norm for her – it was certainly nothing to write home about.

Yet, in spite of the sacrifices they'd made with the less than glamorous holidays, her parents didn't compromise on paying for the training that they hoped would make her a star – and it was a gesture for which Jessie was ever grateful. "I was a normal kid," she added, "[but] my parents invested a lot in me, from singing lessons to ballet costumes. I could never say I had a tough upbringing."

Indeed, by the age of six, her showbiz lust had already stepped up a gear and she found herself attending four classes per week. Most of these were at the Wenn Stage School in Ilford, which was located within walking distance of her home. A young Jessie faced some tough competition there – not only were her older sisters already skilled in dance, but her own classes were filled with talented children too, including the founder's well-trained daughter and niece to name but a few. In spite of Jessie's inexperience, the school's founder, Dawn Wenn-Kober, fell instantly in love with her.

"When you have a big group of kids, sometimes your eyes are just drawn to a particular child and that's how I felt about Jessie – your eyes were always drawn to her," she told the author. "She was a really bubbly little girl – she was really enthusiastic and wanted to do everything. She was always a live-wire in the class – a class with Jessie in it was never boring."

She added: "She was really determined [to beat the competition], bright as a button, very enthusiastic – I would say overly so – and that comes from giving 100 per cent of herself all the time. She clearly had a unique stage presence and she was always keen to try new things."

What was more, there was no rest for the talented – and, even if she'd been feeling shy, she was encouraged to try all of the classes. "She was six so we throw them into everything to see what they're good at," Dawn explained, "but because she was good at everything, she carried on doing everything! She'd say, 'I'm too tall to be a ballet dancer, so I'm not going to do ballet!' And we'd say, 'Yes, you are!'"

Even as a child, Jessie was head and shoulders above her peers and, according to Dawn, was "blessed with incredible legs that just go on and on". Although practising ballet at a young age would stand her in good stead for the future by harnessing her self-discipline and focus, she did struggle at times due to her physique. "She was always tall, with a short body and long legs, which is very difficult when you're little," Dawn recalled. "She was very supple and when your legs are so long, it's quite difficult as you have little muscle power to control them, so they go all over the place."

For a girl whose first words were "jam hot" and who loved the urban music scene, classical ballet tunes didn't impress her much either. "She was all about the music," Dawn chuckled wryly, "and classical wasn't her thing. She didn't want classical dancing either as she would want to do her own style. She also had quite a high instep so her feet weren't as strong as they might have been, although she did practise pointe work. Most kids complain about ballet at some point, but she did try to get out of ballet as soon as she could, or as much as she could."

However, she would persevere with her ballet training for several years longer and – as much as she complained bitterly at times – she even grew to enjoy it. But the one aspect of performance that Jessie lived for above all else was singing. Her parents, whom she described as her "two best mates", also encouraged her early passion for music. The reggae rhythms of Bob Marley, the iconic dance classics of Michael Jackson and the heartbreak ballads and empowerment anthems of Mariah Carey and Whitney Houston were all regulars on Jessie's CD player. Her favourites, though, were soul and funk artists – and there were some that her parents were responsible for introducing her to. "I am so, like, the uncoolest person ever," she joked. "My dad's cooler than me. He was the one playing D-Train and Funkadelic in the house. I will not lie!"

She added to *Gigwise*: "My mum and dad would always have music playing, some funk and soul, thank God they had good taste in music. I grew up listening to Funkadelic, The Gap Band, Aretha Franklin, Prince, Michael Jackson and James Brown."

Less credible was an "obsession" with The Spice Girls. Jessie had wanted to be Posh Spice as a child, but felt that she "wasn't pretty enough". However she defended her lack of credibility and her right to play the good, the bad and the embarrassing, telling *Global Grind*: "The best thing about growing up in a family that loves music is that you get everything from TLC to The Beatles to Michael Jackson to Tracy Chapman – music is beautiful because it doesn't all sound the same. You know, I always say, how would you fall in love if everybody looked the same? How would music be judged if we all sounded the same? That's the best thing about the music industry, that everyone has their own likes and dislikes."

Jessie also admired the emotional quality of soul music, whether it told of a heartbroken lover clinging to her other half, like Etta James in 'I'd Rather Go Blind (Than See You Walk Away)', an incurable romantic full of craving like Prince in 'The Beautiful Ones' or an emotionally overwrought lover at the end of his tether who's turning away from relationships altogether, like Bob Marley in 'No Woman No Cry'.

What was more, to her, music had no colour. While she felt some of the other white families in her town were borderline racist, blaming immigration for their troubles, Jessie was the polar opposite, believing music to be a universal language that could break any barrier – and that included race and colour.

To complement her musical diet, her parents encouraged her to be creative with what she'd learned by enrolling her in private singing lessons every week. However, she was no ordinary singing personality. Unusually, despite being a keen ballet dancer, Jessie was also becoming a self-confessed tomboy. Like Rihanna, who would later go on to straddle a bright pink cannon ready for war in her music video 'Hard', Jessie would also play with gender, mixing up the male and female – with often disastrous results. "I wore a plastic flower on the side of my head with a bun, a blue Gap jumper, tracksuit bottoms and shell-toe trainers," she cringed to *Bliss* magazine of her preteen fashion efforts. "I literally lived in that outfit for a year!"

While Rihanna would combine a fierce scowl or a jacket decorated with lethal-looking spikes with thick black eyeliner and undeniably feminine sex appeal, Jessie too was interested in blurring gender boundaries. Not only that, but both were perceived to have been boyish as children.

"I wasn't someone who played with dolls or did the typical girly things," Jessie told *PrideSource*. "I was always the girl who was a bit ballsy and quite rebellious and I always had something to say. You know how some girls were all like, 'Everyone's lovely and I love everything?' Well, I was kind of like, 'No, I don't like that.' If I wanted to play football with the boys, I would… I didn't care if I looked stupid or my nail split. I wasn't that kind of obsessive girly Barbie doll."

Perhaps it wasn't surprising that Jessie was a little boyish – from day one her father encouraged all three of his daughters to unleash their inner tomboy. In a bid to toughen them up and hone their survival skills, he persuaded them to sleep in a tent in their back garden from time to time in the summer. To liven things up, he would often create potentially fatal scenarios for them to escape from, such as pretending to be a wild bear invading their camp. He hoped that this would train them to prepare for the emergencies of life.

Whether or not the bid had succeeded, what it did do was spark off a longstanding phobia of camping. Jessie elaborated to *Q* magazine: "When I was a kid, my dad used to make me and my sisters sleep in a tent to man us up a bit. All I have is a memory of my dad weeing in a bucket outside, him pretending to be a bear, getting really bad heat rash and eczema… my mum taking pictures from the house going, 'Hi kids!', being really eccentric."

Her experiences of camping had left her hot, sweaty and miserable – tents infested with woodlice hadn't helped – and instead of the great outdoors becoming the fun place to play that her father had hoped, it became the stuff of nightmares. "I think that's why [I can't do the tent thing any more]," she later shuddered. Not such a tomboy after all – sleeping out under the stars might have practically been part of the Cornish family's bloodline, but Jessie was loathe to join in.

In spite of the hiccups, she enjoyed a close relationship with her father. The two would regularly travel to tube stations, where they would "randomly" dance or sing together in full public view. They would also joke around constantly; despite having an emotionally draining job as a social worker for disadvantaged members of the community, her dad believed that laughter was the best medicine – for the privileged and under-privileged alike.

"At Christmas, it's a competition in my whole family as to who can make everyone laugh the most," Jessie told the *News Of The World*. "My dad, my sisters and my mum are comedians." She regularly won the contests by pulling cartoonish and cross-eyed faces, an ability she'd inherited from her dad. The harmony at home seemed almost surreal. However, in spite of an idyllic home life, filled with laughter and happiness, Jessie's world was about to be marred by a tragedy that would change life as she knew it forever. What was more, she was just eight years old.

It had started out as a day of fun like any other. "Me, my dad and my sisters were in Epping Forest and my dad said, 'Let's race to the car,' Jessie recalled to *The Telegraph*, "and I just collapsed."

At first the others had thought Jessie, the youngest in the family and the most notorious prankster, was playing a practical joke – but this was no April Fool's stunt. "They were like, 'Stop messing around!'", she continued. "But I just went white and got rushed to hospital."

Once there, she was diagnosed with Wolff-Parkinson-White syndrome, a debilitating heart condition that can cause sufferers' heart rates to increase by up to four times the normal speed. Symptoms include chest pain, palpitations, a pounding heartbeat and a temporary inability to breathe. Sufferers can also experience such intense dizziness that they faint. Obviously, the human body has just one electrical pathway in the heart, purpose-built to regulate the heartbeat and to prevent it from becoming too fast. However sufferers of Wolff-Parkinson-White syndrome have an extra pathway, one which – if triggered by physical activity or stress – can spiral out of control. It was a lesson that Jessie had learned at a cruelly young age.

From the moment of diagnosis, her life was one of rules and restrictions. Ahead of her should have been the archetypal experiences of late childhood – illicit sips of alcopops, playing kiss chase in the park, racing each other in the playground, climbing trees and scaling fences, or girls taking on boys for a gender-wars football game. Yet now she couldn't run or even ride a bike without fear. What was more, even when she did feel strong enough to do intensive exercise, her terrified parents banned it, fearing for her safety. Her father in particular was very protective as he knew from direct experience what the dangers were – her heart condition was a genetic one. "I remember my mum and dad saying, 'You're just like daddy, you've got a special heart,'" Jessie recalled. "Every time I got sick, my dad [would feel] so guilty, like it was his fault. He's got Wolff-Parkinson-White syndrome [too]. It's just one of those things."

In a bid to prevent the onset of more attacks, her father put a healthy eating regime in place. "My mum would make me fake McDonald's because she never wanted me to have it," Jessie chuckled to Global Grind. "She would make me chips and do some nice healthy chicken and put it in a box and put an M on it and I used to be fooled every time!"

Her mother would also sing to her to shake the depression, play her favourite soul tunes on repeat when she tired of singing herself, and gently remind her that her problems were not as bad as she thought.

"[My bad health] never really hindered my love of life, because my parents never really let it," she continued. "They would be like, 'OK, there are people way worse off than you'."

In spite of their optimism, adjusting to life as a child who would never be the same as her peers wasn't easy. Most painfully of all, she was forbidden from taking part in school sports lessons in case the exertion triggered an attack. While she'd previously been an active child, she was now reduced to standing on the sidelines, watching wistfully as her classmates competed. Fiercely competitive and driven even at her laziest, it wasn't Jessie's style.

To add salt to her wounds, her school's Ofsted report berated pupils for not being more physically fit, one of the few major problems they wanted the school to tackle. No matter how much Jessie might have wanted to be more active, it was never going to be a reality – and it was a bitter pill to swallow for a boisterous child full of excess energy. "I couldn't really be as free as other kids," she lamented later. "I always had to take it slow, otherwise I'd end up [ill]."

The carefree, liberated, reckless Jessie, who had shared the same devil-may-care attitude as most of her friends, had gone forever. Now one wrong move could see her back in hospital – and it wasn't a risk she was prepared to take.

However, Jessie soon drowned her sorrows in music and performance and, encouraged by her equally ambitious ballet dancer mother, her desire to take to the stage stepped up a notch. She was no longer content with ballet and tap classes on the weekend or passively listening to the musical greats she admired. Coming face to face with her own mortality at such an early age defined Jessie's goals and gave her a focus – she could no longer take life and good health for granted, so she wanted to achieve as much as she could. "I would watch the BRITs and say 'Mummy, I want to be her, be that person and win an award!'" Jessie recalled. "My mum said: 'One day you WILL be there and win it.'"

Encouraged by her optimism, Jessie found herself auditioning for lead roles in school plays like *Annie* – one production a young Amy Winehouse had also been part of a few years previously. However, a class of eight-year-olds weren't ready for what a thrilled Jessie had to offer. "I was just loud since the age of eight," she remarked wryly to *The Big Issue*. "They didn't let me into the school production of *Annie* because I was too loud."

Jessie had boasted a formidable voice, but back then it had been more of a curse than a blessing. She was mortified when, at the casting, every single one of her friends made it through – apart from her. "Everyone got in – there were literally like 100 of them," she told VEVO, cringing at the memory. "When it came to me, they were just like, 'Sorry' and I walked out on my own."

It could have been that Jessie's tutors feared she would overshadow her peers, who might not have been able to match the strengths of her voice – but, as a child, it was a bitter disappointment and a despondent Jessie fought with herself not to take the snub personally. "I didn't do plays in school [after that] because I didn't really feel comfortable with not being accepted, and not everyone used to like my voice," she vented to PopEater. "People used to tell me to be quiet and laugh at my songs when I'd write songs." However, she soon learned to take the situation in her stride, adding: "I believe a song lasts forever. It's the best up-yours you can possibly give."

The *Annie* audition was just one in a string of humiliating rejections – later, even Jessie's request to join the choir would be denied – but it would prepare her for a life in showbiz, giving her the thick skin she needed for survival in a cut-throat industry. It might have been embarrassing in primary school, but as she grew older, standing out from the crowd would prove to be the best thing she'd ever done.

Undeterred, Jessie turned to TV, finding her match in advertising slots on the children's TV channel Nickelodeon. Meanwhile, in her spare time, she began putting pen to paper and devising her own songs. "I remember going to her house when we were younger and she kept a box full of the songs she'd written," fellow aspiring child actress Natalie Green told the author. "She was always really ambitious, even back then."

Yet it was the first song Jessie ever wrote that meant the most to her. While her rival Lady Gaga's first song – devised at age 13 – had been sweet and innocent, inspired by her orthodox Catholic father's classical music collection, Jessie's had a much darker twist – she'd been subversive from the start.

Gaga had written about a love that had been lost and how the lovers might find what had attracted them to each other in the first place and rekindle the flame. Back then, her parents had provided a diet of princesses in fairytale castles meeting their handsome princes and living happily ever after – without thought of illness, poverty or any of the other battles of real life. Plus her neighbourhood had been upscale New York, not the bullet-dodging, knife-wielding culture of downtown Romford with its East London overspill. Unsurprisingly then, her first work was that of a hopeless romantic. A far cry from her later, much more subversive, work, Gaga had been motivated by misty-eyed childhood idealism. Jessie's, however, was motivated by reality – and her life so far had been much less romantic. "I was nine," Jessie told *The Mirror*. "I don't really talk about it much because it's pretty bad – 'There is never freedom in a world like ours, people always dying, what is it all about?' – and I was nine! Seriously intense child."

Yet she'd hit on a winning formula. As macabre as it might have sounded to a child, The Black Eyed Peas had a worldwide hit years later with 'Where Is The Love?' which dealt with exactly the same topic.

However, Jessie's song had probably been inspired by Michael Jackson's 1995 hit 'Earth Song' or his 1996 tune 'They Don't Care About Us', both of which had very similar themes or lyrics to her own song. Dealing with death, poverty, rampant evil, the needless suffering of children and the self-destruction of the human race, his songs were even less cheerful than Jessie's.

What was more, another thing she shared in common with Michael was her hatred of racism. Jackson had later admitted that the dramatic scenes in the 'Earth Song' video shoot, featuring him sinking to the floor in incandescent rage while miming the words "What about us?", had been totally authentic and unscripted. The famous scenes had been a reaction to his genuine fury both at the suffering depicted in the song lyrics and at his own life events – including being a victim of racism.

Yet while Michael hadn't covered the perils of racism directly and explicitly, using more diplomatic phrases, such as it not mattering whether a person was black or white, Jessie tackled it head-on in her very first song.

"One of the biggest motivations for it was definitely her anger at racist behaviour," an anonymous friend revealed to the author. "She had black and mixed-race friends all her life and she had no time for ignorance. Jessie would call it colour blindness. In her eyes, intolerance is acceptable if you're allergic to a food – not when you have an issue with someone because of their race." The friend added: "Plus the fact, she had a real affinity with people of colour because she thought they had natural rhythm in their blood. Most of the artists she grew up with

– all the kings and queens of soul – were black, so she always had really positive things to say about people of colour. She grew up with them in her bedroom, coming out of her speakers… treating them differently never entered her head."

Years later, Jessie would put her disgust at intolerance into words publicly, telling the BBC: "I want young people to know that they can belong – whatever your culture, your religion [or] your sexuality, that you can live life how you want to live it and feel comfortable how you are."

In spite of brief flashes of brilliance musically, Jessie's life was still blighted by her rapid heartbeat, which would flare up from time to time and see her sent back to hospital. Jessie's medicine cabinet was full, but her attacks kept returning – and it wasn't long before specialists suggested trying a permanent cure. Jessie underwent harrowing cardioversion – a procedure where electric shocks are administered to the heart – in hope of a solution.

An incision is normally made in the sufferer's groin, from which a tube is inserted into an artery directly leading to the heart. Radiofrequency energy then burns away the affected area. Undergoing a radiotherapy treatment, just as a cancer victim might, terrified Jessie – but it was her best hope. "I had some wires put into my shoulder and my groin and into my heart," she recalled to *The Mirror*. "They tried to zap it into a normal rhythm, and it didn't really work."

Her only other hope for a permanent cure was open-heart surgery – but due to the high mortality rate and huge risk of complications, this type of surgery is usually reserved for extreme cases. In any case, Jessie was terrified of going under the knife – and she had good reason to be. While she was in hospital, her wardmate – just a young boy – had the same surgery for a heart transplant and never woke up. "I was in Great Ormond Street hospital, opposite this little boy," she recalled sorrowfully to *The Big Issue*. "I remember waking up in the night and hearing him pray [for God to save his life]. He was on his knees with all these wires hanging out. He passed away the next day and I remember asking my mum why God didn't save him."

Perhaps his prayers had been answered after all – his death had brought an end to his pain. But for a young Jessie, his death was not just a shock, but a grave injustice. "One day he was there and the next he was gone," she explained incredulously.

Perhaps it was hardly surprising that Jessie was an "intense" child – in fact, her trauma also led to the onset of OCD. While she struggled to come to terms with the indignity of children dying young, she was expected to enrol at Mayfield Secondary School in Dagenham. This would spell a dark time for Jessie – one that would soon see life getting even worse.

She would struggle under the weight of expectation from the moment she arrived. She wasn't a blank slate – her two elder sisters had already set a standard in school and made the family name notorious. They were both renowned for being straight-A students and had been respected head girls with their names on a plaque in the assembly hall. Unfortunately for Jessie though, she just wasn't academic – and no amount of burying her head in the books was going to change that.

"I was never really that good at anything," she told *The Independent* despairingly. "At school, they were like, 'Oh, you're a Cornish girl!' and they kind of expected me to be the same as my sisters. Give me something to draw or an outfit to pick for someone or hair, make-up, acting, write a song, I'm fine with it, but anything to do with sums – it was never my thing."

While Jessie would later say that she had never based her intelligence on her exam results, there were times when being different still got her down. "I cried because I wasn't doing well at school and all my friends were," she told *Bliss* magazine. "But my mum, dad and sisters always made me feel comfortable."

However, in the school environment, she couldn't turn to her family – and she sometimes felt lost among all of the high-flying achievers. She would descend into depression, knowing she would never be academic and that it wasn't what she aimed to do with her life.

To make matters worse, instead of being praised for her vocal abilities – the one thing she did feel confident about – her teachers criticised them. The school was less than sympathetic about her penchant for breaking into song to liven up the more boring classes – and, increasingly, she found herself accused of being disruptive. "I was so bad at history, maths, science, geography, anything academic," she told MTV. "I really tried, it just never clicked with me. Every single report was, 'Jessica could do with not distracting people with her voice.'"

Even in situations where singing was acceptable, Jessie never fitted in. Within a day of joining the school choir, she was banned from it altogether. "I was in it for a day and some of the adults were moaning that their kids were upset that I was too good. I was 11. Can you imagine? I was heartbroken."

Before long, a devastated Jessie had grown to doubt even the voice she had been so proud of. "I'm not the best singer around," she later told the *Daily Mail*, before conceding: "At school I wasn't good at maths or science but I *was* a decent singer. I have to believe in myself. If I don't, then who will? I won't apologise for who I am."

But back at the tender age of 11, Jessie hadn't yet harnessed that self-belief – and when she didn't measure up to her sisters or her peers, she suffered from crippling feelings of inadequacy. According to an old acquaintance, school had by then become little more than a prison sentence.

"Jessie was the underdog at school," she revealed to the author. "She was quiet and kept herself to herself with a small group of friends who were just as modest and quiet as she was. She wasn't the prettiest or the cleverest and she really didn't stand out from a crowd. Back then, she wasn't that confident, so I would never have guessed she'd be a star. At the time, she was just really sensitive and because music hadn't taken off for her yet, I think she worried she'd just be seen as a less accomplished version of her sisters and end up living in their shadow for ever more."

The ways that Jessie did stand out, however, were all for the wrong reasons. She had often been dubbed "out of this world" – but not for her striking voice, which was still deemed "too loud" by disapproving adults and disdainful classmates. Like her idol Rihanna before her, who had been told off for singing too loudly in the bath, her voice piercing through the thin walls of her modest Barbados home and angering her neighbours, Jessie too struggled to win favour with her sound.

To her peers, she wasn't "out of this world" because of how she sang – but because, to them, she looked like an alien. "I was called 'alien' because I had a heart problem, so I had these beta-blockers that actually turned my skin green," Jessie recalled to *The Big Issue*. "At the time, [the bullying] was horrific."

As attempts to cure her heart defect had failed, Jessie needed the medication to save her from repeated attacks or, perhaps, even to save her life. Yet, as she was learning, one of the most prominent side effects of the drugs was daily torment from her classmates. Even her sticky-out teeth made her a target.

Jessie had begun high school as an ambitious, attention-loving drama queen and a self-confessed "show-off" with a strong sense of self – someone who had conquered her heart defect to live a normal, happy life. But her confidence wasn't to last long.

Jessie was counter-cultural and, perhaps to some, intimidatingly different and self-assured. She just wasn't one of the pack. It was her uniqueness that would later bring her success and attention on the stage – it is essential for a pop artist to be different in order to stand out from the crowd and earn an otherwise elusive record deal. Yet back in her schooldays, being different wasn't a signature of being special – it was a direct invitation to be picked on.

It wasn't long before Jessie was falling prey to cruel remarks. According to an anonymous classmate, the school bullies temporarily "killed who she was". While the acquaintance knew Jessie only in passing and was neither a friend nor an enemy, she had seen the effect of the bullying. "She started out as a radiant girl with a lot of energy and she was more opinionated than most. But people laughed down her opinions, I think, or sometimes just ignored them altogether. She started to feel like a square peg in a round hole."

Her early schooldays were also lonely at times. Her classmate continued: "She would sometimes get snubbed at lunch breaks, so she'd be left sitting on her own with no one to talk to. She did have a group of friends, but sometimes people would be friendly to her face, when it was just the two of them, but in front of others they'd slag her over to win favour in front of the ringleader or to win status from the more dominant girls in the group. That's all they cared about and they'd pick her up and drop her when it suited them, so she started to rely more heavily on her family, I think. Bullying her upped other girls' social positions, so if they felt insecure about their own place in the group, they'd be mean about her. Jessie never really knew who her friends were or who to trust."

She added: "People who did want to target her for the really nasty stuff were crafty about how they did it – they wouldn't want to get caught by a teacher, but they knew once they were out of the school gates and no one in authority was watching, they could get away with what they wanted. They would follow her and throw stones at her. It was really sad to see. She ended up blending in and trying to hide away. They eroded her confidence and made her afraid to be herself. She became a total shadow of the happy-go-lucky girl she'd once been. They killed her fighting spirit – but, thank God, not for long."

Chapter 2

Take A Look At Me Now

"If I fall over, if I wobble, if I can't do it – I will just sing!"

Jessie J

Indeed, Jessie soon bounced back. Against all odds, being too loud had turned out to be a blessing in disguise. It was exactly what would attract Andrew Lloyd Webber to the 11-year-old when she was cast in the first run of the legendary West End musical *Whistle Down The Wind*.

Landing the part of someone called Brat might not have seemed glamorous to the non-theatrical world, but Jessie was thrilled – and it was the perfect opportunity for her to start using her voice.

Finally she had found an outlet for the talents that set her apart from her sisters and saved her from her perpetual position in their shadows. While she didn't have the temperament for studying that her sisters did, she knew that they didn't have what she had either. "My family is very creative, but no one in my family sings," Jessie later told *MusicRemedy* of her light-bulb moment. "I was the only one who put my life to a melody."

Whistle Down The Wind first came to life in Washington, D.C. in 1996 and was based on a 1959 book of the same title by Mary Hayley Bell, which was adapted for a movie two years later that starred Alan Bates and Bell's daughter Hayley Mills, who was 14 at the time. The musical was bound for Broadway, but – following a stream of negative reviews – it never made it to New York at all. Its planned run across America was cancelled, amid shock that a production with the Lloyd Webber name had failed. Instead of being the household name the team had hoped for, it was a laughing stock.

After taking time out to lick their wounds and heal their bruised egos, the producers reactivated *Whistle Down The Wind*, this time in London, with an 11-year-old Jessie on board.

In a bid to reinvent the musical and add a little more street cred this time round, an album was recorded by celebrity guest artists featuring cover versions of every track in the musical. Singers such as Boy George, Bonnie Tyler, Tom Jones and Meat Loaf were part of the album, although the most famous contribution came from Boyzone. Their cover of 'No Matter What' was released as a single that year and it instantly went platinum, hitting the number one spot in 18 countries and becoming the highest-selling song ever produced from a musical in chart history. The tables were really turning for *Whistle Down The Wind*.

Revitalised by its West End makeover, it made its UK debut at the Aldwych Theatre in London's Soho. A tender comedy with a serious edge, the plot involved a family of bereaved children and their hopes that a stranger they are hiding at their home - who due to a misunderstanding they believe to be Jesus Christ but turns out to be a murderer on the run – has the power to bring their mother back from the dead.

The first major song during the musical was 'Never Get What I Pray For'. In it, Jessie and her companions are fantasising over all the things they crave but fear they'll never have – from the childlike longings for lipsticks and kites, or teenage-era cravings for a dance with the best-looking guy at the school prom, to adult aspirations to be "beautiful, sexy and smart" and to look like movie star Doris Day.

After bemoaning their lack of money and superficial things, their thoughts turn back to what they really want, the return of their deceased mother, the only thing money can't buy.

Performing this track every night for two years running put a seed of inspiration into Jessie's head that would one day go on to become the song 'Price Tag'. She took the message that life wasn't simply about the material things to heart and, like these children – due to her health scares – she was learning at a surprisingly early age that life was more precious than money.

Poignantly, the next move in the plot is to rescue a litter of neglected kittens, who have been left for dead in a sewer, and set them free, symbolising that saving lives was more important than saving – or spending – money. As the children make their way back to the trailer, lesson learned, they break into the song 'Home By Now' about the place where their hearts lie.

Jessie related to the message – as a victim of bullying, stress and over-intense academia, school had been a prison for her. Yet home was her safety net, somewhere she could go when life got her down.

However, the play then took a twist that, thankfully for Jessie, she couldn't relate to. The family haven't been home for long when they encounter a runaway criminal hiding in their barn. When they approach him and ask who he is, his only response is to sink to his knees and breathe "Jesus Christ!" Unbeknown to them, he is not the son of God, but a murderer on the town's most wanted list, yet – blissfully ignorant – Jessie and her two stage sisters promise to keep him safe. Empowered by his arrival, they soon break into the anthem 'Children Rule The World'.

Alongside the fiasco in the barn is the ultimate taboo – a doomed love affair between a black girl and a white boy who know that, against a backdrop of America's repressed, conservative Deep South, going public will always be forbidden. Later in her life, Jessie would also fall prey to forbidden yet insatiable love and find herself misunderstood as a result. For her, she knew she would always "fall in love with someone people disapproved of" due to her emerging sexuality.

As the tragic love affair plays itself out, the children keep the murderer on his toes with an increasingly ludicrous list of requests. They ask him to tell them stories from the "next Testament", quiz him on the injustice of death and beg him to resurrect their mother from the dead. Even when the would-be Jesus is outed as an intruder and burns down the barn in a dramatic finale, the children are still convinced that he could have been God's son, imploring: "But how do you know?"

For two years, Jessie would wish away the hours at school by day before rushing to London's West End every night, where she became Brat. However, *Whistle Down The Wind* was Jessie's first major performance – and, before she could revel in the glory, she would battle to conquer terrifying stage fright. In fact, she'd been so nervous there were fears at times that she wouldn't make it on to the stage at all.

"She was absolutely petrified," revealed Dawn Wenn-Kober to the author. "The stage manager called me to say, 'Could you just come and boost her confidence?' so I went down to reassure her. She had to be really nurtured and encouraged to get into it – but when she got bitten by the bug and realised how good she was, there was no stopping her!"

Jessie's infamous enthusiasm would sometimes overtake her – and, on one occasion, the wrong footwork sent her flying into the crowd. "There was a scene at the end of the show where they were standing very close to the front of the stage and she went to move to the back when she literally just lost her balance and fell backwards into the pit," Dawn chuckled. It was an accident that would earn her the nickname Brat Pitt.

Jessie had an equally colourful memory of events. "I was singing 'Children rule the world tonight!'", she recalled to *The Telegraph*, "and as I hopped to go offstage, my foot went into the orchestra pit and I did a back flip on to the conductor. I was, like, splattered over the orchestra – sheets of music everywhere!"

According to Dawn, the accident alerted health and safety to change the structure of the theatre. "It was because of Jessie that they now actually have a grille over the orchestra," she told the author. "And Andrew Lloyd Webber sent her a book of his musicals as a gift with a note saying, 'So sorry you had an accident, here's a token of my appreciation for your performance.'"

However, in Jessie's eyes, there was a very different reason for his kindness. "I think he was worried I was going to sue him," she joked. "He really cosied up after that." It turned out to be just one of many awkward moments for Webber, who would later find himself publicly humiliated by fellow outspoken Essex girl Denise Van Outen when he cut her from the judging panel of his show *Over The Rainbow* after she fell pregnant.

Fortunately for him, Jessie wasn't one to hold a grudge. Tumbling backwards and falling headfirst into the orchestra in front of thousands at her first ever West End musical might have deterred many girls – let alone one with a heart defect – but Jessie refused to be beaten. In fact, she had to be restrained from firing the understudy and racing back out. "She wanted to continue the show, even when she fell," Dawn recalled, "but they insisted that she went to hospital and got checked out. She was saying afterwards, 'I wanted to go back on and finish, I wanted to so much but they wouldn't let me!'"

She was later able to make a joke out of it, chuckling: "They all used to call me Brat Pitt, because I fell!" She added: "That's when it all started – you can get paid for this? Bring it on!" Being paid for painful falls wouldn't seem ideal to many but a rather masochistic Jessie found pleasure in self-discipline and resilience.

A tenacious Jessie had also learned how to keep her stage fright at bay. "I think she got it because she's an absolute perfectionist and she has to get it just right," Dawn recalled. "She kept thinking, 'What about if I get that note wrong?' Playing Brat was a major role and it was a lot to remember as a child – you've got to master the choreography, get the right lines, interact with the people – there's loads to learn."

Not only that, but while Jessie had been praised for the freestyle acting she'd done as a child, she now found herself forced to conform to the restrictions of being Brat – being Jessica Cornish was no longer enough. "You can't do your own thing," Dawn explained. "There were three children playing Brat on each cycle and so all of them had to do it exactly the same – there was no manoeuvrability. She had to do it exactly as it was, so I'm sure there was an element of 'Will I do it right?' – but Jessie turned out to be one of the best Brats they ever had."

Jessie's fears hadn't been unfounded, though – she was up against some accomplished child singers such as Dawn's daughter Kirstie Kober and a boy named James Buckley, who would later go on to star in the TV show *The Inbetweeners*.

She had no outrageous costumes to hide behind, no budget-busting pre-recorded videos and, most importantly, no Auto-Tune. She'd be showing her talent live and in its rarest form. Back in the days when she was just Jessica Cornish, a girl from Romford with insecurities like no other – and, to top it all off, a heart defect – fame had seemed daunting. She was still fighting to find her place among the other equally competitive, determined fame addicts – and hoping to come out on top. But despite her insecurities the storyline of her first musical would inspire her to pen what would one day become a chart-topping hit.

Yet *Whistle Down The Wind* would prove to be a good training ground for Jessie. She began to come alive as Brat, realising she'd finally found something she was passionate about. "I think that made me grow up really fast," she related to *The Independent*. "It made me realise that I could do what I loved and be paid for it."

She added to *I Like Music*: "I think [that was when] I realised music was for me… I could hang out with adults and just be on stage and have that buzz. I started to realise I could make my hobby my career. I could get paid for it and I could pay my parents back for the ballet shoes and the costumes. I think that's when it hit me that I wanted to [be in showbiz] even though I was quite young. It was also around that age that people started to realise that my voice was a lot stronger. I don't know if it was good then or if I was just really loud. I think I was just really loud!"

However, Dawn disagreed and, recognising Jessie's potential, began to invite her round to her family home to pit herself against the strongest singer in school – her daughter. The two would battle to outdo each other in a bid to be both the loudest and the best. "She was duet partners with Kirstie many times," Dawn recalled. "They would try to out-sing each other and together they were amazing, just really going for it."

Jessie was also encouraged to take additional singing classes, where she would learn about harmonising, microphone techniques, how to read music to produce the correct pitch on demand and how to breathe while singing. The Wenn website claims: "Producing the correct pitch [is] a skill that can be learned. Many of our best singers started with us because our parents were suffering as their child was 'tone deaf'!"

However, that was one problem Jessie had never had – she was a natural from the start. According to Dawn, she'd had a clear, strong and tuneful voice from the age of six. However, what the classes did was teach her how to make the most of her talents. "Her vocal coach struggled to get her to develop her technique correctly as we could all see she had a very unique voice – very powerful with a lovely tone – and we wanted to make sure her voice was safe, as we thought she'd go down the musical theatre path [in her career]," she recalled. "Her teacher would challenge her quite a bit – 'You must sing in this way, otherwise you're going to ruin your voice – you're not going to be able to sustain this for hours and hours without damaging it', because her voice had such power."

In fact, her voice would prove so powerful that it saw her win the British Arts Awards twice. The awards were part of an annual ceremony run by the British Arts Trust, which had worked to improve the standards of performing arts across the country since the Second World War, when its founder had taken to the stage at prisons, military camps and soldiers' barracks to entertain. In the 21st century, they had become a little more glamorous, seeing hopefuls perform their dance, drama and music recitals at major arenas instead.

In 2000, Jessie beat thousands of other entrants to the finals with her rendition of the old jazz standard 'Summertime' – a version so powerful that it would give mentor Dawn Wenn-Kober "goose bumps" of pride. Urbanite Jessie performing a jazz standard was about as likely as seeing heavy rock group Metallica perform at a tribute concert for S Club 7, or seeing Lady Gaga perform in a pair of jeans. Yet, according to Dawn, this unlikely match merely gave Jessie an opportunity to show off the versatility of her voice. "That was an amazing feat of control for Jessie because you have to sing it in classical style, absolutely as it is," she revealed. "You can't do your own twist to it, so it was a fabulous way for her to show off techniques that she had learned." That year, she won the competition.

Not only that, but she got her own back on the tutors who'd banished her from the school choir when she was invited to be in a much more prestigious one, as part of the Carmel Thomas Youth Singers. The founder both owned a theatrical agency and taught choir at local Essex schools – and, based on her professional expertise, she believed Jessie had everything it took.

In August 2000, she flew a 12-year-old Jessie out to Germany with just seven others, whom she believed were Britain's brightest singing talents, to take part in the European Youth Musical Festival's Kinderchoir. The festival showcased three million children from 5,000 schools across the world and Jessie was proud to be representing the country and showing the haters she could sing after all.

There was more good news in store for Jessie. When Wenn started to cast for its annual musical production, she was singled out by examiners as outstanding and landed a top part in *Bugsy Malone*. "We hired outside people to cast for us to make it fair as my niece and daughter were in the running," Dawn recalled. "We did some audition tapes and asked, 'Who do you think?' They came back with my daughter and Jessie, saying they were really exceptional individuals. They said, 'They've really got something and we could have watched them all day!'"

Consequently Jessie found herself part of *Bugsy Malone*, a child-friendly account of the tough gangland culture of inner-city New York. Although the musical was modelled on the infamous exploits of notorious Prohibition-era gangsters like Al Capone, it was a light-hearted comedy take on their world. Instead of bullets, the guns shot custard, while one gang shunned weapons altogether, retaliating with pies. There were no deaths either – only a great big mess.

Jessie played Blousey, a would-be starlet facing hiccups on the road to success. While her last part had seen her take the role of a materialistic, tantrum-prone spoiled brat, she would now be playing her polar opposite – a painfully shy singer with little appetite for the guns and violence around her. Cursed by a mixture of inhibition and plain bad luck, she's too sensitive to play the fame game and invariably ends up hurt. She attends auditions and is on the brink of winning a rival singer's place after she storms out, only to see her return and thwart her efforts. At her most despondent, after her lover falsely promises her a trip to Hollywood to further her career, she sings the solo number 'Ordinary Fool', lamenting how she thinks with her heart instead of her head. As the show ends, Blousey is ever hopeful, but no closer to achieving her dream.

Jessie had had enough painful life experiences to accurately channel Blousey, a frustrated artist who'd once sung that her dreams always fell through when "a road I've walked before ends alone at my front door".

A modern-day Blousey may be Big Brother wannabe Chantelle Houghton, who is most memorable on the reality show merely for pretending to be famous; someone who has since desperately tried to find love but has ended up kissing frogs, whose biggest selling point is a facial similarity to heiress Paris Hilton and whose career highlights are ribbon-cutting at Essex branches of lingerie shops like La Senza. Her life – together with bulimia, an unhealthy dose of self-loathing, an alleged addiction to cosmetic surgery and a series of tearful meltdowns in public places – has ended up emblazoned across the pages of tabloids, when – as a starry-eyed girl – all she'd ever wanted was "to better myself". What was more, the perils of growing up in public were apparent – her every mistake was documented in a national newspaper.

Jessie too seemed bewildered and her eyes painted an authentic picture of a little girl lost, but for her it was just acting and she would later go on to fulfil all of her dreams.

For now though, clad in a painfully unfashionable long lilac coat and matching hat, she'd be Blousey – the girl whose dreams always fell down.

"Blousey was a very nervy and understated part which she played gently and with great sympathy for the character," Dawn recalled. Not only had she been successful, but the year she played Blousey – at age 12 – would be the very last time she would ever succumb to stage fright. "That went out of the window when she realised she could do it," Dawn continued. "The opening night of *Bugsy* was the last time she ever got it. Once she got on stage, it was gone and she was loving it. Anyway, first-night nerves are good for you as it keeps you focused and gets your adrenalin going."

For Jessie, her jitters had suddenly seemed small in comparison to the tough blows childhood had already dealt her. While her classmates had been busy with binge drinking and boyfriends, Jessie had been lying in a hospital bed, contemplating open-heart surgery and watching her wardmates die in front of her eyes. Her school friends might have been choking on their first cigarettes, but Jessie had been battling attacks so intense that she'd struggled to breathe at all – smoking had never been an option. And while the biggest threat most of her peers faced was being reprimanded for forgetting to finish their homework, Jessie had already stared death in the face. Nothing could faze her now – and stage fright was the least of her worries. A newly fearless Jessie was giving every stage show her all.

What was more, in a further bid not to be defeated, at age 12 she was attending Grade 4 ballet classes while hooked up to a heart monitor. A high-pitched alarm would sound to warn her if her heart rate spiralled out of control, an awkward impediment for any child, but – as she'd been taught by her stage-school parents – at all costs, the show had to go on.

"There was a time when she had to wear a heart monitor to check her heartbeat – definitely some difficult times and we were very worried, but Jessie just took it in her stride," Dawn recalled. "We did a fundraising show to raise some money for the unit of Great Ormond Street Hospital where she stayed. It was scary times for her – she was never quite sure if she'd had a heart issue because she was panicking or just because she'd been dancing. She had a couple of funny turns, but because she played it down, everyone else played it down. I'm sure in her head it was affecting her much more than it showed [but] we always taught our pupils 'the show must go on.' That's the mentality of the industry."

Some of the preteen pupils, however, weren't quite as au fait with Jessie's fighting spirit. "We were open-mouthed with shock when she walked in with the monitor," an anonymous classmate told the author. "We were really frightened something was going to happen, in case her dancing triggered an attack. I think to be honest we were more tense than she was! She never made a fuss and never wanted to be treated 'special' because she didn't want the sympathy vote from playing the sick child. She was really modest."

Indeed, Jessie's condition had only made her all the more determined to succeed. "One time, when she was doing a particularly difficult section of ballet in an exam where you have to stand on one leg and twirl, I remember Jessie saying: 'If I fall over, if I wobble, if I can't do it, I will just sing!'" Dawn chuckled. "I told her, 'That will be very lovely, Jessie, but I don't think it'll get you through the exam!'"

She added: "Her enthusiasm sometimes overtook her, but she was always very disciplined and she had a clear idea that, some way or another, she was going to perform."

The following year, Jessie proved that to the public again when she won the part of the cat in the musical *Honk*. Based on the fairy tale *The Ugly Duckling*, the show was a musical comedy with a moral tale about celebrating diversity. The storyline sees an unusual-looking duck hatch from an egg, only to honk instead of quacking as expected. He is made the object of ridicule by cruel bystanders from that moment onwards. Running away from the bullies who degrade him, the duck soon finds himself driven into the path of Jessie – a ruthless, predatory cat with murder on her mind.

This time, Jessie was playing the part of the bully, taking on the mind-set of the very people who'd been unkind to her. She was stalking her prey in the hope of inviting him back to the "Kitty Kat Shack" for a bite to eat. That tasty titbit, of course, was him. Dodging the cat's hungry jaws, the unfortunately named duck, Ugly, falls in love with a beautiful swan. Then disaster strikes and he finds himself frozen in snow. The warmth of his distraught mother's tears thaw him out, however – and he returns to life as a handsome swan, who can be with his love after all.

The play, which had been seen in more than 8,000 productions across the world, including in Japan, Iceland, Israel and Australia, was praised by the *Evening Standard* as "cracking entertainment". Meanwhile *Time Out* described the show as "the best Christmas show ever [with] dazzling choreography". It continued: "Imagine the colour and wit of Disney's *Jungle Book*, mixed with the vivacity of '40s Hollywood musicals, exuberantly staged and you still only have some idea of how stonkingly brilliant this Christmas treat is."

Not only did the production achieve rave reviews, but it appealed to Jessie's respect for diversity. Director Anthony Drew explained of the moral: "The theme of the show is the acceptance of others who may appear different for whatever reason. In our increasingly multicultural society, school bullying, racism, sexism, homophobia, ageism and any other "isms" you care to mention are still prevalent. The main message that we wanted the audience to go away with is that being different is okay – it is something to be welcomed, embraced and celebrated rather than feared, misunderstood or persecuted."

This was a notion an already misunderstood Jessie would welcome. She'd fallen prey to bullies, was technically set apart from others due to a disability and – even at her early age – had already felt stirrings of girl-on-girl crushes. She wasn't exactly the average child. Knowing the anxiety being different could bring, she later went on to echo the message of the play when she told the BBC: "I want young people to know that they can belong – whatever your culture, your religion, your sexuality, that you can live life how you want to live it and feel comfortable enough how you are."

What was more, Jessie was beginning to live her own message. Performance had given her the confidence to break free from the bullies in her own life. As an anonymous friend from Jessie's high school later told *Now* magazine, "the taunts had become almost unbearable as she entered her teens". In an unusual twist, she claimed that – although Jessie had played the cat in *Honk* – she had actually been seen as more of an ugly duckling.

"Jessie was quiet and looked really geeky and plain at school," the friend revealed. "She could never get a boyfriend and was really unlucky in love. While all her school friends were starting to have relationships, she was already left out. She was so shy, she wouldn't say if she fancied someone because she knew it probably wouldn't be mutual. She was an easy target because she was so quiet. Her tormentors seized the opportunity to tease her for the tablets she had to take. They called her 'alien' for years due to her medication, which turned her skin almost a shade of green."

Not content with E.T. comparisons, her bullies also ridiculed her prominent teeth – something which ironically saw both friends and foes label her Bugs Bunny. While her friends were affectionately teasing, however, not everyone was joking – and she would still have to dodge the rocks and stones classmates threw at her when she passed.

Yet Jessie was liberated by life on the stage, a place where she could express herself without being shy. The stage became her safety net – and so did her home. What was more, after talking to her family, she began to re-evaluate what her bullies were doing. "My dad always used to say to me that people who bully, there's a reason for it and it's actually because they're the insecure ones," she told the BBC. "It says more about them than it ever will about you and that's something that I think a lot of young people don't realise, is that a bully is a bully for a reason. They're not bullying you because of you, they're bullying you because of how THEY are."

Growing up in a loving family also healed Jessie's hurt. Her parents were still together, which, in a country where almost half of all marriages at that time ended in divorce, was to her more the exception than the norm. "They're the best mum and dad you could ever wish for," Jessie gushed. "They're still together, which is super-rare. They go on dates and are still in love and they very much set the standard for me about what treating someone good is."

Meanwhile, Jessie became an anti-bullying campaigner herself. She had a culture of self-help around her – Dawn, the founder of Wenn Stage School and a close friend of her parents, was a counsellor for the National Association of People Abused in Childhood (NAPAC), while Jessie's father was a social worker who had talked desperate teenagers out of suicide as part of his job. Inspired, Jessie later told the BBC: "I want to create a place [on the internet] where, when someone types in online 'How to kill myself', that comes up and it's a place of hope instead of a place of darkness."

Before long, however, Jessie was even being bullied in the showbiz industry. As they grew older, her peers had become increasingly competitive and she found herself facing their jealousy when she succeeded. She was sickened by the bitchiness of rival performers, the ruthless and cut-throat nature of the industry and the threats that an ever-turning rumour mill seemed apt to provide. Her worst fears had come true – even performance was no longer enjoyable.

Secretly she longed to break away from the stage and become a politician, but she feared she "wasn't clever enough". Either way, she felt her stint in showbiz had come to an end. She didn't want a life of catfights and petty jealousy, but her "pushy" stage parents felt otherwise and insisted that she perform. "The best thing about my parents is that they kind of push," Jessie told Global Grind. "I remember when I said I didn't want to do performance any more and my mother said: 'Not cool.' I was 14 and I told her I didn't want to do it any more, you know, I got tired of the girl pacts and the favourites and the politics of it, even when I was that young."

However, her family wasn't taking no for an answer – and demanded that she continue. According to Dawn Wenn-Kober, their determination for her not to waste her talents was Jessie's saving grace. "She is blessed with sensible parents who have their feet firmly on the ground and they ensured that she did work and it wasn't just fun and games," Dawn recalled. "[It was] years and years of hard slog and her parents made her stay grounded. She would say: 'Do I have to do ballet today?' and they were like: 'Yes, you do!' The strict rules of ballet helped her to create her own self-discipline."

Jessie's feet would have been bruised, swollen and bloody at first and her pointe work was no mean feat for a young child – especially someone who didn't even want to be there – but she persevered. Having been told in no uncertain terms that bowing out wasn't an option, Jessie had no choice but to continue. "The only reason I ever carried on was for my mum and dad and my family because we're a family of fighters," she recalled to *I Like Music*. "My mum and dad taught me never to give up. I'm a go-getter."

Instead of quitting, she stepped up her game even further, enrolling in a second stage school. She took dance and drama classes at the Collins Performing Arts school in Essex, where she and comedian-to-be James Buckley would meet again. His most enduring memory of her had been as a geeky, awkward 11-year-old plunging headfirst into the orchestra in *Whistle Down The Wind* to peals of laughter from the audience – hardly a flattering first impression.

This time, however, sparks flew and the pair became the best of friends. "James was a right laugh," Jessie recalled fondly to *The Sun*. "He was the naughty one with all the cheek in classes. The teachers used to try and give him a telling off but you could tell they were laughing along with him."

She would later out a shame-faced James as a secret dance fan, teasingly revealing to the paper: "He was in some dance classes with me, but he would kill me if I told you more about that."

She hadn't stopped attending her main school, Wenn, either, where she would sing in corridors, and, seeing her passion for it, the founder's niece, Christina Cuttell, recommended someone to her who could help. She was raving about a producer she'd met who'd made all of her recording fantasies come true and given her her very first album. She passed on his contact details and, in February 2003, just a month before her 15th birthday, Jessie followed suit.

Arriving at a cramped garden shed in Maldon, Essex, her first taste of a recording studio was far from glamorous, but this visit to a makeshift studio was to be the start of something big. The name Soundmagic Studios might have conjured up thoughts of a deluxe facility crammed with miracle-working recording equipment, but although the reality was very different, it was enough to manage Jessie's expectations. In fact, it would make her dreams come true.

Music enthusiast Steve Tsoi had left an engineering position at Ford two years earlier, where he'd been managing a team that designed car parts, to focus on producing his own band. While the security of a regular income was vital to support his wife and two children, he'd decided to take an enormous leap of faith to make his hobby a career.

The business had instantly prospered, although by the time he met Jessie, he'd still been operating out of his back garden. Undeterred, she had booked a six-hour session with him – then priced at £150 – to record a 10-track CD.

The six-hour marathon was labelled as the "Platinum Experience", which Steve described as "the ultimate session for [already] confident singers". Jessie was certainly confident. In fact, it was a session that would reduce her formerly sensible father to tears.

"She came with her dad," Steve told the author, "and she wanted to do a day's recording to make a CD she could use to promote herself. That was the goal. She was quite a slim girl and when she started singing, my chin hit the floor and I just wondered where that massive voice came from. It was so mature for her age. Her dad, Steve, who was in the control room with me, started crying out of pure joy. He'd obviously heard her singing before but not at such close quarters and he was moved by the whole experience."

Her producer was open-mouthed, her father was tearful and Jessie herself was just elated. The session had confirmed to her that singing was the career she wanted. She had performed 'Against All Odds' by Phil Collins, 'Out There On My Own' (a track from the musical *Fame*), 'Hero' by her idol Mariah Carey, the old jazz standard 'Get Happy', which had been covered by numerous artist, the Bette Midler tracks 'From A Distance' and 'Wind Beneath My Wings' and 'Get Here If You Can' by Oleta Adams. She'd also belted out 'Perfect Moment', the tender first single of soap star turned pop performer Martine McCutcheon, and a song that was a regular fixture among Jessie's classmates, as well as 'Torn' by Australian performer Natalie Imbruglia and finally 'Whistle Down The Wind', the title track of her first ever musical.

Jessie spent the first four hours of her session recording the songs before going to the Compasses pub in Maldon, while Steve worked on post-production, mastering and mixing the tracks. Fortunately for him, compared with some of the hapless hopefuls he'd worked with, there was very little work required.

"As soon as she came through the door, there was no doubt she could sing," Steve told the author. "I see a lot of teenage wannabes who think that they can sing but can't and managing their expectations is really difficult. One woman came in to do a whole bunch of Whitney Houston songs, and had it in mind to launch herself as a tribute act. It was an okay performance, listenable, but she wasn't Whitney Houston. She came into the control room afterwards to listen and then she said: 'Okay, over to you now.' I said: 'What do you mean?' and she said: 'Make me sound like Whitney Houston!... What do you mean you can't? You must have a Whitney Houston button on there!'"

As it turned out, she would be bitterly disappointed – no amount of Auto-Tune was going to turn her into her favourite soul singer. But not only was Jessie a "really pleasant and personable teenager" with no such expectations, Steve found himself in a position where he barely had to work his magic on the songs at all.

"I didn't do anything special to her recording voice to make it sound better," he recalled. "If I'd done 10 songs with someone who wasn't as good as Jessie, I would have needed much longer. In fact, I wouldn't let that person do 10 songs as we'd be limited by time. The Whitney Houston wannabe would've needed six hours of post-production with 10 songs, whereas Jessie only needed an hour and a half."

What was more, Jessie had only needed to do two to three takes for each song, while the average client had taken four or five. In fact, he liked the samples so much, the standout track 'Against All Odds' was immediately posted on his website. This was a tough selection procedure, with just one in 10 of the would-be singers deemed good enough to have their work showcased in this way.

Jessie's stage school beginnings had seen her use intense focus and discipline to comply with specific characters or sounds and be able to sound like them exactly; instead of stamping the songs with her own identity, she'd focused on trying to sound as similar as possible to the original recording. "She didn't make them her own," Steve explained. "She didn't do an Eva Cassidy, whose version of 'Over The Rainbow' sounded completely different. That wasn't the purpose of recording; it was just for Jessie to showcase her talent to take her to the next level."

Jessie was delighted with the results – and even more so when she heard 'Against All Odds' would make the website. "The song struck me as being different," Steve recalled. "I tend to only put up things that are good and out of the thousands of recordings we've done, that definitely stood out."

When Jessie had booked the sessions, it had been partly for an ego boost and partly to entice record labels and music producers to notice her. However, as soon as the sample hit the net, it became clear that she had a potential sideline for a career in performance already.

"When I put the sample up, I lost count of how many emails I got from people saying: 'What a voice, could I get Jessie to come and sing at my wedding or birthday party?'" Steve recalled. "I forwarded all the emails to Jessie just saying, 'Do you wanna do it?', because I didn't want to become her agent! She could probably have made a living out of doing that even back then. I got at least a dozen emails for her, compared to none for everyone else. She was the best person we had on our website, easily." He added: "I can't think of anything I would call a weakness."

This was glowing praise indeed for a girl who, less than a year before, had been on the brink of giving it all up to become a politician. "I think the MPs – Gordon Brown and co. – would probably have breathed a huge sigh of relief," an old classmate joked to the author, "because Jessie was back in the best business there is – showbusiness."

'Against All Odds' had opened the floodgates for a possible career, but it had another special meaning for Jessie. She might have sung it in the same style as the original, but she definitely re-interpreted the meaning. It had been written about an ill-fated relationship that the songwriter is desperate to resurrect, despite knowing that being together again now would be near impossible – "against all odds".

However for Jessie, the words "take a look at me now" weren't a plea to an ex-lover to take her back into his heart, but a defiant retort to the people who'd bullied her in childhood. They might have thought a life of medication, heart monitors and misery in hospital beds had rendered her incapable of reaching her dream. This was her verbal retaliation to the stones they'd thrown. In fact, she felt so strongly about the words that she chose them for her album cover.

She wasn't the first recruit Steve had worked with who'd wanted to get their own back. "The studio appeared on a TV show called *Would You Dump Me Now?*, which gave people the opportunity to do something they had always wanted to do, but never had the chance to – to show people who'd jilted them at the altar what they were capable of now. For one girl, it was recording a CD. She'd had a physical makeover so she looked completely different and really confident, then she recorded the CD, brought the guy in and said: 'Would you dump me now?' It ended up on Sky, on the Wedding Channel."

Just like the jilted brides on the show, Jessie was getting her own back on her detractors and proving that she could be a star. However, for her, it wasn't just a revenge bid – wanting to be famous was a goal that now consumed her whole life. Even as she left the studio with the CD in her hands that she felt might be a golden ticket to fame, she was breaking into song.

It was ironic that Jessie's big break would come at a time when she'd been about to quit showbiz altogether. It was even more so because she would achieve her break by entering a show similar to The *X Factor* – the one thing she'd always said she would shun.

She would later tell *Metro* dismissively: "For me, *X Factor* is something that's entertaining. I wouldn't say it was a path I would have chosen. I always feel I would much prefer to work for something." She added: "I don't like getting anything unless I have really worked for it and I feel like I'd be skipping the queue if I went on *X Factor*." Years later, she would audaciously tell Simon Cowell the very same to his face – and he would commend her for being "feisty".

Dawn Wenn-Kober had been equally dismissive of the show, claiming: "I don't think any artist that's got the amount of talent that Jessie's got would ever go on *X Factor*."

Despite growing up in an era where shows like *Big Brother* gave fame-hungry – yet often talentless – contestants an instant platform from which to launch their careers, and one which saw *Pop Idol* and *Britain's Got Talent* hopefuls (often desperately in need of Auto-Tune) get booed off the stage for painfully bad renditions of popular songs, Jessie had other ideas. Yet, at age 15, she went against all of her reservations and entered a televised singing contest in the hope that it would bring her notoriety, recognition and fame.

In 2003, the BBC was appealing for talented children to apply for an awards show that would put under-16s in the spotlight for musical, academic, sporting or other achievements. That show was known as *Britain's Brilliant Prodigies*. Jessie sent in the CD she'd recorded at Soundmagic Studios and a thrilled TV team called and invited her to audition.

Jessie had been panicking about whether or not the CD was good enough – after all, aside from rapping with school friends in a basement garage, it had been the first time she'd ever set foot in a recording studio. Even if she did have what it took to be a star, would the CD represent that? What was more, how would she perform on the night, knowing that if she got a slot on national TV, she would potentially be singing to millions? The pressure was on. Yet, sure enough, she earned a place in the finals.

Jessie would be singing 'Against All Odds' for the show – a Phil Collins song which Mariah Carey had covered in 2000 both as a solo version and as a joint effort with the boyband Westlife. Ironically, *X Factor* winner

Steve Brookstein would use the song as his debut single less than a year after Jessie performed it on the show.

She was competing to be the UK's "Best Young Pop Singer" while other categories included "Best Young Instrumentalist", "Best Young Sports Person", "Best Young Classical Singer" and – bizarrely – "Best Young Chess Player".

To most viewers, it was just a TV show like any other, but Jessie's parents were glued to the screen. The BBC website summarised: "Britain's Brilliant Prodigy Awards are like the Oscars for the young and talented. They are given out to teens who make a difference and whose achievements show other young people they can do what they want if they put their minds to it."

An ex-member of the pop band Steps had posted a message of encouragement on the show's website, cautioning: "You have to be really determined and keep training but, above all, you have to believe in yourself."

Back then, Jessie had not been a fan of "cheesy" pop, preferring to be a soul diva at heart. While she'd recorded some of the same songs on her CD as her friend Christina Cuttell, she'd omitted tender anthems like 'I Turn To You' by Christina Aguilera and popular preteen ballad 'Never Had A Dream Come True' by S Club 7 – and she'd admitted that she found Disney songs "irritating".

Although, under those conditions, Jessie was unlikely to pay special attention to the words of a Steps singer, she recognised the importance of believing in herself. Years later, she told the BBC – appearing not as a child prodigy award winner, but as an already accomplished singer with a number one single – "You have to have confidence. If I walked on stage apologising and saying: 'Okay, I'm going to sing – I don't know if it's going to be any good or not', people would be like: 'Wait a minute, if she doesn't believe in herself, why should we believe in her?' My family and friends have always said: 'Believe in yourself, because if you don't, no one else will.'"

Jessie needed a dose of self-belief to compete against the other hopefuls. One, Seb Clover, had made a solo trip across the Atlantic Ocean, battling to avert disaster when marauding whales he'd described as "roughly the same size as the boat" drew too near and threatened to capsize it. He would go on to be the overall winner of Child Prodigy of the Year.

Meanwhile, in Jessie's category – Best Young Pop Singer – while she'd fought off competition from hundreds of would-be child stars to make it to the final six, she was still up against some pretty tough competition.

That evening, in May 2003, she made it, winning her category. Surrounding herself with confident people, applying a confident mind-set and repeating the self-help mantras her father swore by had paid off. Even as a teenager with a conservative mousey brown hairdo, baggy white trousers and a modest, loose fitting khaki vest top, she was posing for pictures with a BBC-awarded trophy – a prize she'd received from Bee Gees member Robin Gibb.

Among those proudly waiting in the wings was Dawn Wenn-Kober. It was a double moment for her as another of her students had been presented with an award by Paul McCartney. However, Jessie had stood out for her audacious onstage claim that she would be back before they knew it – with a chart-topping hit. "When she collected the award, she said she hoped she would have a number one single," Dawn recalled, "and the presenter said: 'Not much of an ambition there, then!'"

Her critics might have rolled their eyes, but little did they – or Jessie, who was talking on adrenalin-fuelled bravado – know that, in a matter of years, that was exactly what would happen.

Chapter 3

Fighting Bullets With Beats

"Music is my drug – and the only drug I'll ever want."

Jessie J

W here next for an aspiring 15-year-old Essex girl on the brink of being discovered? If you're from upper-crust Kensington, stereotypes dictate that you enroll at a place like the Sylvia Young Theatre School – and beg, wheedle and cajole your parents into paying the fees. However, formidable fee structures of several thousand pounds a term would quickly rule out the working classes.

According to the stereotypes, just two types of girl attended this school – those who scrimped, saved and sacrificed or those with multimillion pound trust funds and seemingly limitless bank balances – people for whom a career was not a financial necessity, but merely a way to pass the time.

Hollyoaks actress and sometime girl-band singer Jodi Albert was in the first category. She had persuaded her cash-strapped parents to remortgage the family home to give her a chance of winning celebrity status, while her father resorted to taking an extra job, working as a taxi driver at all hours just to pay the bills. However, this self-sacrifice was not symbolic of all parents – and not everyone could wrap their families around their little fingers.

Down-to-earth middle-class parents, on the other hand, sent their children to the BRIT School, the only fee-free performing arts school in the country. It was state funded and received regular cash injections from within the music industry, too. Its reputation was a little more rough and ready than the archetypal stage school, with plaques of green mould streaked up the walls of the nearest railway station and beggars ever-present in the surrounding Croydon streets.

However, thanks to the BRIT School, the town was also home to numerous creative types. The hallways were filled with drama kings and queens parading their fashions and showcasing their personalities and styles. There were the bohemian types with indie hairstyles, moody gazes and skinny jeans so tight they looked as though they might have needed surgical removal. Many sported fashionably messy hairstyles which, despite looking deliberately unkempt, often took great effort to perfect.

In contrast, the glamorous fame-hungry divas had barely a nail out of place. They sported stilettos, glitter and – on really flamboyant days – black velvet elbow-length gloves and burlesque-style head feathers. These types – and everything in between – could all be found at the BRIT School.

And not only was it fashion forward, but it also offered good career prospects. The brochures boasted: "If an applicant is determined on a life devoted to art, dance, music, radio, television/film or theatre, then this could well be the right place."

What was more, its alumni list read like the credits of a music festival. The school had been home to Katie Melua, The Kooks and The Feeling at the start of their careers. In fact, a nameless band had once existed there consisting of The Kooks' guitar player Luke Pritchard, lead vocalist Katie Melua and future *X Factor* winner Leona Lewis, who back then played keyboards for the trio. It was all the persuasion Jessie needed to apply for a place.

Of course not everyone had glowing references for the school – a fickle Amy Winehouse would attend for just three weeks before denouncing the place as "shit". Radio 1 DJs would rave that Amy's brief flirtation with stage school had put Croydon on the map, but her reciprocal praise for the school was much more muted, seeing her declare to the press:

"I hated it." Meanwhile one of her tutors would merely shudder that she "wasn't suited to being institutionalised".

A focused Jessie was undeterred by the debate. Far from an elitist institution, the BRIT School was open to all and, while competition was intense, a third of all applicants would be granted entry. Her prospects on graduation seemed promising too, with former pupils having become actors in West End musicals, record label bosses, touring stage dancers, stars of TV dramas and even sportsmen making it big as Premier League football players. Jessie's goal was simple, however, and it was listed on the prospectus. A lucky few who studied here would go on to make "award winning albums".

In March 2004, a few days before her 16th birthday, Jessie made the journey down to Croydon to audition. She'd filled in an application form for a post-16 BTEC diploma in musical theatre, answering mandatory questions such as: "What do you think are the five most important skills for a musical theatre performer?", "What makes a musical commercially successful?" and "Think of a musical you have seen and describe how you would stage it differently if you were a director." Having passed that part of the selection procedure, she now had to show her skills in person.

The musical theatre course gave equal weight to dance, drama and singing skills, and so Jessie was tested in all three. Fellow BRIT School pupil Kerry Louise Barnaby was at the auditions with her. "For drama, we had a choice of three monologues," she told the author. "We had to memorise one of three chunks of text from a play and perform it and then they'd ask questions. They were open to interpretation, so they'd ask, 'Why did you decide to do that play and to perform it the way you did?' Then there was a jazz dance workshop – they taught us a routine that we had to perform – and finally there was singing. If you were good at two of the three, you were in."

Jessie passed all three, wowing judges by singing standards such as 'Wish Upon A Star' – and she was invited to enrol that autumn. While she waited for her dream course to begin, she auditioned for *Evita*, but was rejected for being "too young".

Soon afterwards, however, she won a starring role as Rose in a local production of *Titanic*, where she played a wealthy musician en route to

America who falls in love with a penniless ship-hand. The future looks bright for the unlikely couple until tragedy strikes and the ship hits the iceberg, sinking into the ocean on its maiden voyage.

No sooner had she finished channelling Rose – the accomplished showbiz star she hoped to be herself one day – than her first term began at the BRIT School. Jessie meant business, and she made sure that first impressions were striking – so much so that her classmates mistook her for a teacher.

"I remember the first time I saw Jess," Kerry Louise Barnaby told the author. "We all thought she was a teacher at first because she walked in with this air of effortless confidence and she was like, 'I'm going to sing now!'"

Her style sense was equally effortless, seeing her sport the same mousey brown hairstyle she'd worn all of her early life. She didn't dress to impress clothes-wise either, sticking to loose-fitting casual threads – but, according to her peers, she could still command the room's attention as soon as she stepped on the stage.

"When she first came, she didn't have a fringe – her hair was just long and straight," Kerry revealed. "She didn't wear much make-up. She'd wear skinny jeans, a plain baggy T-shirt and Converses. That was it, that was Jess."

While she'd made an impression on the BRIT School, what impression had the BRIT School made on her? It certainly wasn't for everyone. Amy Winehouse had moaned to the press later about the lack of eye candy, claiming: "I was like, 'Where's the men? What is going on?' So I used to lock myself away and just do music, because I hated the school. Every lunchtime, every break, I'd be up in the music room playing a guitar or piano."

Jessie was equally reclusive – but for very different reasons. Not only were most of her male friends gay, but she was beginning to question her own sexuality too. In any case, music meant so much to her that a lack of male company was the last thing on her mind.

Aside from that, like Amy, Jessie struggled to fit in at the school and find her niche among the fun-loving drama student types. It was a time of experimentation for many of them, in which a passion for drama combined itself with one for drinking. Yet Jessie was purposeful – a woman with a seemingly preordained plan. "People were talking about going to drama school after they left," Kerry revealed, "and she was like, 'I don't need to do that – I'm going to sing', like it was already planned out."

While the others were enjoying their first taste of adulthood and freedom – and were in no hurry to grow up just yet – Jessie already knew what she wanted to do and was dead-set on that goal, often at the expense of socialising.

"Jessie was very focused, almost focused to the point that she didn't want to have fun," Kerry claimed. "She thought fun was a lack of focus."

Not only was she seen as a stick in the mud, but alcohol issues also came between her and her classmates. Teenage hedonism had always been impossible for Jessie due to her heart condition – and her absence from the drunken nights out created a rift.

"Because she never drank, she never got involved socially," Kerry continued. "She used to look down a bit on people who drank – and we drank a lot. I remember one day when I was up drinking until 7 a.m. and I went to a rehearsal at 9 a.m. Everyone was saying: 'Are you drunk?' but then my tutor told me: 'That's the best performance you've ever done.'"

Unfortunately a more serious Jessie didn't agree – and, according to Kerry, she began to spread rumours that a friend was an alcoholic. The offender had arrived at school with a bottle of vodka in her bag for a party later that day. "She would seem to feel like, 'You're not as good as me because you feel you have to drink'", Kerry claimed, "and we were like, 'No, we don't have to, we're 17 and we're at drama school and we wanna have fun!' Anything that was construed as having fun, Jessie looked down upon."

Whether or not Jessie really was the disapproving party pooper she was portrayed as, she did live a life of purity, abstaining from alcohol, drugs and tobacco altogether. "I was in and out of hospital most of my childhood, but it was a blessing in disguise. It meant I could never abuse my body the way my friends did at 16, drink myself into a frenzy or smoke weed when everyone else was trying it," she confirmed to *The Mirror*.

However, some felt that it wasn't just her health problems that turned her away from living hard. "Jessie had such discipline and focus and this steely determination all the time that even if she'd had nine lives and a replacement liver on standby, I doubt she'd have touched alcohol anyway," another anonymous friend commented. "She just wasn't on that level and it would never have been her scene."

Jessie later added to *The Independent*: "Life is too short to intoxicate my body with booze and drugs. I never got into that dark side of the world like so many people do."

However, unfortunately for Jessie, alcohol was such a big part of student culture that she found herself feeling increasingly left out. Not only that, but she faced a three-hour round trip by herself each day, as she'd chosen to stay in Essex and live at home – a disaster for any new student's social life.

"I had to travel in from Romford to Croydon every day," Jessie recalled to *I Like Music*. "I did six trains and I had to get up at 5 a.m. every day for two years. It made me really independent, to be able to do that every day and travel and know where to go if the Central line was closed. It was a big daunting thing for a young person. I remember not really being able to have a social life. Everyone else at school would live there."

Perhaps in her heart, there was a sense of injustice that at 5 a.m., while the girls who might have been her close friends under different circumstances were clubbing the night away, she was 50 miles away from them, yawning, rubbing her eyes and pressing snooze on the alarm clock, dreading another long commute. While the others might have reluctantly changed out of their micro miniskirts into something a little more demure for the first morning's lecture, a then quiet and less than glamorous Jessie would put on her trusty Converse trainers and a reliable pair of jeans, just as she did every other day.

However, even if she had felt she was missing out, she hadn't wanted to sacrifice her home life. "I commuted because I needed to have that home thing," she explained to *I Like Music*. After a traumatic childhood that had seen her yo-yo in and out of hospital, home was a place she could go to recuperate – and the loving atmosphere of family life would heal her pain, while strengthening her for the fame game that lay ahead.

"I had my moments, as every teenagers should," she confided to *Bliss* magazine. "At some point everyone should have been like: 'Argh, I'm stuck, I don't know what to do!'" However, Jessie's moments were sometimes worse than most. "There were times when I cried... because I didn't have the best outfit, but my mum, dad and sisters always made me feel comfortable."

In fact, the healing power of home was so profound for Jessie that she even wrote an early song about it. "One of the first songs I wrote was called 'Sky Is Her Home' about myself when I was younger," she continued. "There were all these things that were going on but when I went home, that's when I felt as if I could spread my wings and be me."

However her absence from school outside of lessons was noticed, and some of her classmates were confused. "She isolated herself," Kerry claimed. "BRIT School became our home, it's where you live. Even if you only had one class, you came in for the whole day. But Jessie was never around. She came in for class and went home."

Yet Kerry had also noticed Jessie's good relationship with her family, and believed it was one of the keys to her success. "Everyone knew she'd make it," she recalled. "She was talented, she was focused and she had a family that were willing to support her and that does make a difference. They would go to the end of the earth for her and do anything to make her dreams come true. They were like: 'Focus on your writing and we'll support you.'"

Meanwhile, Jessie might not have been known for her debauchery or for downing the most pints at the bar, but she was keen to compete with the one thing that meant something to her – her music. According to Kerry, she was determined to capture attention. "She made sure people would remember her and she made sure she made an impression on us. She didn't care if it was good or bad," she revealed. "She didn't care whether you liked or hated her, as long as people knew who she was."

People did know who she was, and before long she had pop-star-to-be Adele, who was doing the music course at the school, eating out of her hand. "We used to jam at lunchtime and someone would play guitar and we would both just sing," Jessie reminisced to *Associated Press*. In fact, while Jessie's classmates in the musical theatre group would play

51

piano together at lunchtimes, appraise each other's performances and give feedback, she had more of an affinity with the music group, and could always be found teaming up with guitarists.

"Jessie was always a singer," Kerry confirmed, "and people thought it was weird she was in musical theatre." Indeed, even though she'd originally seen herself embracing a life in musicals, gracing West End stages, Jessie was now finding herself drawn to the music strand, and the people studying it.

"Adele was very kind of loud and everyone loved her," Jessie revealed to *Associated Press*. "She was the girl everyone loved and was up for a laugh and you could hear her laugh a mile down the corridor."

The affection was mutual, and Jessie had also won the admiration of future soul singer Katy B, who later told Digital Spy: "Jessie and Adele were both in the year above me and they were singers I really looked up to. They really inspired me."

Fellow student Kelly Kim Kranstoun found Jessie awe-inspiring too, despite being one year her senior. "She has a stunning musical theatre singing voice, pure strength and backbone in her voice with great vibrato finishes and great feeling behind every song," she told the author.

As Jessie settled in and began to earn respect from her fellow students, she started to loosen up and enjoy the experience a little more. "It was amazing," she admitted. "There were always these points where you'd have like a 16-part harmony in the middle of the cafeteria, people singing 'Oh Happy Day', or dancers stretching on the balcony at really inappropriate times. But it was really just a school for kids that wanted to be different, just trying to reach their dreams. It's no different from any other school and there were the kids who did their maths and the English and the sciences, but there was also the other strand of kids that kinda bled away from that, and that's where I did my intervals. The things that I definitely think the BRIT School gives you is opportunity and independence."

Although it was fun, it also had some of the discipline that a focused Jessie longed for, with one girl in the class repeatedly fainting at the gates because she'd run so hard to make it on time to her classroom. Doors would be locked the moment lectures began and latecomers would find themselves shut out for the duration of the lesson. Jessie was a perfectionist who didn't want an environment that allowed her to become lazy or complacent, and the school offered that.

The curriculum had a strong focus on drama, seeing students performing with masks and analysing passages from plays. Dance was also a highlight. "The compulsory stuff was mainly jazz dancing," Kerry Louise Barnaby explained. "Most musical theatre is rooted in jazz. You don't have to be trained for years to pick it up, as it's not as technical as ballet. Ballet would isolate people straight away if they couldn't do it, but jazz is all about portraying a character through your dance. If the technique's not great, but you're still portraying the character right, then it's okay."

As someone who had trained extensively in ballet, Jessie would have excelled at both, but her heart wasn't in it – she now had eyes only for music. "She was one of the strongest dancers, but she didn't do any elective ballet or tap classes," Kerry continued. "Only about a third of people in the year were really any good at dance and she was one of them [but] most of Jessie's time was spent with the music strand."

Music was quickly becoming an obsession, and Jessie had an extreme way of announcing to the world how much she wanted to be a singer. "I used to draw music notes on my face," she told MTV, before revealing she'd once considered having the symbols tattooed on permanently. "I wanted people to know that I was a musician at heart. People always used to say to me [thinking it was a tattoo], 'Is that real?' and I was like: 'Oh, no, it isn't.' I thought: 'Maybe I should get a tattoo for real. Luckily, I didn't! Imagine a music note on my face - that would have been horrific!"

Many famous singers seemed to have had an addiction that they had paid tribute to with ink. For Amy Winehouse, it was her ill-fated love affair with then boyfriend Blake, whose name she tattooed across her heart prior to their tempestuous marriage. Cynics argued that a tattoo of a crack pipe might have been more appropriate, but Amy was loyal to Blake. For Katy Perry, it was a tattoo of Jesus on her wrist – a security blanket she could also go back to if a life of "sordid" stardom failed – but for Jessie it was pure and simple. Even if she hadn't taken the plunge and had it tattooed across her face, music was her only love.

By now, in spite of that, Jessie had a boyfriend who accompanied her to school shows. "They weren't touchy feely, but looking at them, you had the impression that they'd be together forever," Kerry observed.

Her fling notwithstanding, Jessie's heart remained with music, and, by the time she turned 17, she would have already ditched him for a taste of her first girl-on-girl experience. "My mum and dad [knew all about my sexuality] for years and were super cool and my sisters made jokes about it, because they were married with kids and I was the rebellious one," Jessie told *Glamour* of that moment in her life. "I had a girlfriend and tattoos – I was, like, hardcore!"

However, even the excitement of an early gay experience wasn't enough to distract Jessie from the ultimate goal: fame. At school, she began to surround herself with a group of people she thought would make it to the top. "I remember Jessie watching one girl perform and saying: 'I didn't know she could sing like that' in awe. It was like she was seeing her for the first time because she could sing," Kerry Louise Barnaby recalled. "When she decided someone was good, then she would give them the time of day, so it was only a very select group of people who she spoke to."

Being surrounded by ambitious people kick-started her instinct to compete. Not only that, but these girls were attending as many in-house auditions as possible and Jessie was inspired to join them.

"There were so many opportunities," she reminisced to *I Like Music*. "You could audition for girl groups and things and learn your craft while you were still at school. You got to put it to the test instead of being like: 'Right, I'm learning, let me go out and audition', you could do it while you were there."

In fact, the school had partnerships with local management companies and theatre companies who would regularly come to test out the talent. The auditions were open to students from across all courses, but girl group auditions seemed on the surface to be more suited to those who were studying purely music. According to the school's website, Jessie's musical theatre course was more broad-based, had an emphasis on "integrating the performing arts" and was designed "to give equal focus to dance, acting and singing".

However, increasingly Jessie was becoming a music fanatic and leaving her stage-school persona behind. She wanted to go to auditions that redressed the balance and reflected her new-found obsession with the world of recording artistry.

In early 2005, that opportunity arrived. Veteran music manager Raymond Stevenson was putting a group together and was looking for three girls to front a hard-hitting anti-gun campaign. On the day, hundreds of girls tried out from across the school. "There was so much tension in the air that you could cut it with a knife," an anonymous hopeful who'd attended the audition revealed. "Everyone was trying to look their best, sound their best and look as if they'd done it a million and one times before, even if in reality it was their first audition."

Then there was Jessie. She had no shortage of self-confidence and an arresting singing voice, but she was unremarkable visually. She didn't yet have what would later become her attention-grabbing signature hairstyle and, according to those around her, hadn't yet grasped the art of dressing to impress.

Not only that, but she had hundreds of other girls to outshine to win her would-be manager's attention. Unfortunately for her, Jessie failed the audition. "Maybe Jessie wasn't taken seriously because she was in the musical theatre strand," an anonymous friend recalled. "Anyway, they thought she wasn't cut out for mainstream pop. This was at a time when she thought she really wanted to take centre stage and record songs instead of singing someone else's and being on stage with lots of others in a musical. But it was another rejection, and she was devastated."

However, she was in luck – Raymond had a change of heart. After debating the matter with his business partner Lucia Hinton, he decided, however inexplicable it might have been, that there was just something about Jessie he liked. His job was to see the potential behind the flaws and transform the girls he felt could make it from raw talent into polished perfection. In Jessie, he could see that raw ability, something he didn't want to let go of. So, against all odds, Jessie was in.

Ironically, she hadn't even seen herself as someone who could have been in a band. "I didn't really wanna be an artist [before the BRIT

School]," she admitted to VEVO. "I kinda spent my whole life training to be on the stage and I auditioned for a girl group just because everyone else was – and I got in!"

There was no turning back now, but for Jessie, the reasons why Raymond had needed to think carefully about including her would quickly come into play. Her only previous experience of performing to pop music had been dancing to Kanye West tracks like 'Gold Digger' while shaking her ass like the dancers did and mouthing the lyrics. "Every time 'Gold Digger' played, I would try in my own way to be like one of the girls in the video," she later blushed to MTV. "I was never curvy enough, but I would dream of being one of those girls and me and my girlfriends would turn it up really loud and just dance to it."

From miming in her front room to singing in the real world, she was now plunged in at the deep end with girls who knew their stuff. Bandmate Bianca Gerald was already an award-winning singer who'd been presented with a prize for "Most Outstanding Young Voice" in London's Leicester Square. She'd been featured as part of a band on music channel The Box four years earlier and she'd even appeared in *Smash Hits* magazine.

Meanwhile Chrystle Gajadhar knew the ropes equally well, having been in the last 65 out of 10,000 for ITV's *Pop Idol* show. She'd also been part of the BBC Jazz Awards, the London Jazz Festival and a gospel group who'd performed at legendary jazz club Ronnie Scott's.

Finally, Shakira Akabusi had trained at the Sylvia Young Theatre School – somewhere that, like Adele before her, Jessie had never been able to afford.

Between them, her new bandmates were intimate with a collection of music which was bewildering to Jessie, even though at home she'd been brought up well versed in many genres. They could sing to reggae, rhythm & blues, soul, hip hop, soca, calypso, bhangra and – in Shakira's case – even "a touch of wild rock". Where did Jessie fit into their world?

Not only that, but two of her three bandmates had taken the reality TV route to get their music noticed – and Jessie had once denounced people who resorted to talent shows as "fakers" who were "skipping the queue". Whether there was tension, rivalry and disagreement or camaraderie all round, however, the four were forced to put their personal feelings to one side to perform.

Their new manager had been approached by Ken Livingstone, the Mayor of London, and personally invited to come up with a solution to the capital's escalating gun culture. Clinical psychologists, social workers and other outsiders had tried and failed to get inside the minds of young killers and now the government was taking its troubles directly to the streets, looking to the urban community itself for an answer.

The perception in that community was that, while psychiatrists and well-meaning yet far-removed outsiders could theorise all they wanted, there was no one better to target the urban youth than the community itself.

Clinical psychologist Dr Tanya Byron, for example, had worked with children as young as 10 growing up in a world where gun warfare and violence was normal. She claimed: "The brutal truth is that the gun and knife culture is growing and the law in itself is not the only answer to this problem."

It took not just punishment but prevention – a way of reaching angry young people before their gun-lust began – and that was where Raymond came in. His solution was to "use music to attack the disease of gun fashion". Whether young Londoners carried guns as a defence weapon, a status symbol or simply a way to survive on the city's increasingly aggressive streets, Raymond aimed to fight bullets with beats and show that there was another way.

He devised a song called 'Why?' for Jessie and her bandmates – who were by now christened Soul Deep UK – to release as the first single for the Don't Trigger campaign. Jessie wouldn't be paid for the project as it was a not-for-profit venture. All performers would be waiving their royalties and donating proceeds to charities and community projects that aimed to stamp out gun culture altogether.

The Mayor's office provided funding, as did the local police force for Lambeth, a South London borough that bore the brunt of the city's gun crime. This funding would be used to record a three-track EP featuring talented but as yet unsigned artists, along with accompanying videos for each song. The first track, 'Why?', would lead the media campaign and its video would have the most expensive budget. It aimed to reach angry and alienated young people who didn't understand the language of reason, instead using the universal language of music. The video also served to honour the hundreds of young lives lost to bullets in the UK each year.

In March 2005, Soul Deep UK arrived at London's City Hall to star in the video, which was dedicated to brutally murdered preteen Damilola Taylor. It began with a short poem, read out by Raymond, which included the words:"So many things to do, things to achieve, then suddenly I couldn't breathe."

As he spoke, the sound of gunshots rang out symbolically from a passing car. The visuals mimicked the scene of death for one of the recent and most high-profile murder victims – a 25-year-old woman with a plan to be a music promoter whose car was hit by a shower of machine gun bullets as she pulled out of a Kent police station.

Then the voices of 14 relatives whose children were lost to gunfire were incorporated into the video. Each mother introduced herself and described how their sons or daughters had died before asking in voices choked with tears:"I want to know why." It was an opportunity for the women to vent, raise awareness and confront their grief head-on, all at the same time.

The scene would skip to images of young people holding placards during an anti-gun demonstration, followed by council-estate kids standing outside tower blocks rapping for a better future. One lyric spoke of a young woman who had grown up to be 6ft tall but had ended up buried 6ft deep in the ground.

The relatives of the deceased had all seen their children meet a grisly end. One was shot dead at just 21, leaving two daughters behind – one of whom was born just days after his death and would never know her father. He had aspired to be a music producer and had just reached the finals of the prestigious MOBO Unsung Awards. Another man's life had been so entrenched in gang warfare that his funeral had to be attended by armed police to prevent further bloodshed.

Meanwhile, one promising 17-year-old, who had a career in the music industry lying ahead of him, met an untimely end in the River

Brent near Greenford, Essex. He'd been shot in the head and stabbed in the heart.

The footage of distressed mothers was interwoven with the song itself, which featured Soul Deep UK dressed all in black and imploring to know why life on the street was "selling so cheap".

Ken Livingstone attended the filming, along with ex-boxer Chris Eubank and various MPs and senior members of police. After the shoot, Soul Deep UK joined the other performers at an East London recording studio to sing and then mix the tracks. Alongside them was a grime group called South Souldiers featuring soul singer Noel McKoy and an Asian three piece who called themselves Sugar Brown, who appeared together on the track 'Heads Up (Listen Up)'. Finally, 'I Die Everyday (RIP J)' was a third anti-gun song performed by new singer Hayley.

Jessie might have seemed lost in the set-up. She didn't look as glamorous or even as confident as the other performers, but – just as her BRIT School classmates had already discovered – appearances could be deceiving.

Noel McKoy, a seasoned music industry veteran known to many as the "Godfather of British Soul", who counted Chaka Khan as a personal friend and who had jammed backstage with artists like Stevie Wonder, was one of those to be surprised. "When you looked at her, you weren't expecting that kind of voice, cuz she had that little baby face!" he revealed to the author. "I wasn't expecting the voice to be that strong and compelling, but it was striking and powerful, with very good projection and she was very confident in her delivery – she always had that big voice."

In fact, it reminded him of one of Jessie's earliest inspirations: Lauryn Hill. He felt from that recording session that she was a contender for Lauryn's crown. "Jessie had a very very black-sounding voice," he continued. "The way she arranged her melody reminds me of Lauryn Hill because she would use patois to make her melodic – you can tell Jessie is inspired by her too. When Lauryn sings, she sings and spits at the same time and that's what Jessie did."

As well as admiring her singing voice, he also took to her personality. "She was upbeat and friendly and looked you in the eye, so I always knew where I stood with her," Noel recalled. "One girl from Don't

Trigger used to come to my club nights and didn't even say 'Hi' or 'Thanks' but Jessie was always more friendly. She was always laughing and joking in the girl group and she never had an attitude. She was one of those artists you'd always get a smile from, who had a fun, zany personality. She was very sweet when I knew her although the music industry toughened her up a bit later." He added: "Whenever I saw her, she was confident, but you're supposed to be that way, you're not meant to be reserved. You don't get into the entertainment industry from being reserved, not unless you have a sugar daddy."

Jessie, on the other hand, was out there on her own, but her hard work paid off in late June 2005 when the video made it on to MTV Base. It was a big hit with viewers, with one taking to the internet to applaud: "The song not only is beautiful but its message is strong and there are real life situations that happen and with this, maybe those who pull the trigger will think twice when they see those heartbroken mums and see that dreams and lives are destroyed."

It enjoyed a good press campaign too, when *The Mirror* honoured Don't Trigger in a special double-page spread entitled "A Bullet Killed Their Dreams". *The Times* had even more glowing praise, claiming the video more worthy of support than Bob Geldof's Live 8 event for its role in "renouncing gun culture". "More important than raising money is changing attitudes – and not just those of the kids in the gangs," it read. "Within the music industry, there are still many rappers and record executives cynically churning out lyrics that endorse gun culture, misogyny and drugs. That sort of person is just as reprehensible as those who pull the triggers on the streets."

According to the feature, music was capable of stirring up hatred and division – and it wasn't hard to see why the paper believed that. The rap artist 50 Cent featured the almost ever-present sound of gunshot cracks in his music and threats of violence such as filling his opponent's "ass with lead". The rapper, who had been shot nine times himself, featured the explicit opinion in his songs that disrespect, disloyalty or dishonour could be retaliated to with violence.

Meanwhile Eminem had written a song called 'Kim', where he fantasises about murdering his wife before throwing her in the ocean after she cheats on him. American rapper DMX even released a single with a lyric about shooting homosexual men dead.

Opinion was that while the adrenalin of a good beat was pumping through their veins, listeners would absorb a dangerous message about the perks of toting a gun. Power, street cred, sex appeal, respect and social superiority, along with the seductive opportunity to be "top dog" and to be admired by their friends but feared by their foes, might have driven their actions.

However, some music fans were angry that their idols were being used as scapegoats. "It's like when Marilyn Manson was blamed for the Columbine shootings in America, where a teenager decided to blow up his school," an anonymous friend of Jessie's argued. "But that guy was insane. Marilyn Manson isn't a satanist. He doesn't worship the devil any more than Britney Spears does. It's just a different style of sound. Music doesn't kill people, only people do that. I don't want to see respected artists end up boycotted unfairly."

There might have been a debate about whether music was responsible but, whether or not it was the problem, it was hoped it could be the solution. 'Why?' was intended to be the antithesis of the messages that popular pro-gun songs gave out, yet it could still get attention because of its urban flavour. Statistically, the vast majority of gun crime was carried out by members of black or ethnic minority groups, who happened to be the pioneers of urban music.

However, this was where Jessie stood out like a sore thumb. Urban Concepts, the marketing agency Raymond had founded, was defined as a "grassroots organisation which utilises the expertise of some of the country's prolific black artists". The Don't Trigger website reinforced that racial message, claiming: "Urban Concepts pride themselves on the fact that they truly represent the community and this year's campaign reflects this... all genres of black, ethnic and urban music are represented. The [video] also has scenes of conflict resolution, which is appropriate when you consider the escalation of gun crime within the black, ethnic and poor communities."

Would viewers find it patronising or perhaps even alienating that Jessie, as a white, middle-class artist, was attempting to understand their situation? What was more, did Jessie herself feel that she didn't belong? She was the only white face in Soul Deep UK and she was one of just a couple of white artists across the entire campaign. Plus, with a background in jazz dancing, ballet and classic musical theatre, Jessie had started out about as far from urban as it was possible to get.

If she felt uncomfortable or marginalised, she would feel even more so when one reviewer from *The Times* wrote: "For white middle-class middle-aged types like me to condemn [gun culture] is useless – which is why it's important that the Don't Trigger campaign has come from the black music industry itself."

Back in 2005, white rappers such as Devlin and Professor Green were yet to come out of the woodwork, and the mainstream urban and hip-hop scene was almost exclusively the domain of racial minorities. Eminem was the only famous counterpart Jessie could compare herself to. While N-Dubz singer Fazer would later rap that just because he was black didn't mean he couldn't be equal, Eminem was sometimes sneered at and dismissed for being "a white rapper". It was as though the two communities hadn't integrated or accepted each other fully and there was still some tension on the music scene – did Jessie feel like a spare part? According to Noel McKoy, she took it all in her stride. "It was mainly a black set-up, sort of multicultural, but she was very comfortable being around black people," he told the author.

Yet while Noel praised her "black-sounding voice", which he felt slotted her into the urban music-based campaign perfectly, not everyone felt the same. While multiracial groups featuring both black and white members would later proliferate on the music scene, in the mid-2000s there was more segregation.

Later, Wretch 32 would feature Example on the single 'Unorthodox', N-Dubz would launch as a multiracial three piece and Dizzee Rascal would team up with blue-eyed Scottish dance act Calvin Harris on the hit 'Dance Wiv Me'. However, general opinion at the time dictated that white rappers and white soul singers were not always seen as authentic. Amy Winehouse, meanwhile, who'd also been applauded for a black-sounding voice, was the topic of hot debate when allegations were made that she was inferior to many black soul artists in her shadow and had merely been released to "put soul into a commercially friendly package that would appeal to a mainstream white audience".

Fortunately for Jessie, she dodged the controversy, finding that she experienced no negativity for her colour. She later told That Grape Juice: "It's been nice how every single culture, walk of life, race and country have really accepted that I grew up on a lot of different music, much of which was soul. I think that stereotypical thing of 'Oh, she's a white girl singing soul music' has gone now." She added: "I think that everyone's matured and music isn't ignorant any more... I am definitely someone who's been influenced by black music."

Jessie seemed confident that she was understood – yet there was more criticism to come. "She comes from such a loving family that she probably couldn't relate to what the others were singing about and why people get on the streets and into gangs in the first place," one of her acquaintances told the author. "People get into gangs because they don't have family – the gangs become their families. They act out all their rage and frustration about their real families or their problems at home, knowing that they have the framework of the gang to protect them from any repercussions. There's one point in the video where Chrystle leans against Jessie, obviously moved by the subject matter and she looks close to tears, frankly. But Jessie just seems detached."

While her heart was in the right place, Jessie wasn't universally accepted and once again she found herself treated like a square peg in a round hole. A flurry of public appearances followed the release of the video and, with them, came more controversy.

The first video screening took place at the Soho Hotel in London, a meeting place for journalists that was the mecca of the media world – and somewhere that was guaranteed to pull an audience of reviewers. A red carpet event in Leicester Square followed, as did a Birmingham church service where hands were joined in forgiveness to the troubled young people who'd pulled a trigger and taken a life. One tearful mother was welcomed with rounds of applause as she announced she'd finally been able to forgive her son's killer and the services were described by those who attended as "sombre" yet "uplifting".

However, one event in particular stood out. There had been an almost funereal atmosphere. While mothers were crying hysterically and even the mayor was reduced to tears, Jessie took to the stage wearing a "raunchy" leather and PVC fetish outfit – and she stood out like a sore thumb.

The event had started out like any other. "Most people were dressed down in suits as it was a remembrance occasion for mourning and celebrating the lives of those kids who'd passed," Noel McKoy told the author. "A few mothers had come on to explain the situation about losing their sons, loads of companies like Mothers Against Guns – and most of them had lost their child to gun crime. It was a really sombre occasion. Ken Livingstone said in his speech: 'I can't imagine how broken these people are', then he went quiet and started crying. It looked very sincere to me." It wasn't exactly the place to showcase a new outfit – in Jessie's case a skimpy, shiny leather-look ensemble with silver bondage-style buckles and a thigh-skimming skirt section.

"To me, it didn't seem the occasion," Noel continued. "I remember people commenting that for an evening of awareness for the mothers, it wasn't appropriate. There was Ken breaking down in his speech, with all these dignitaries, these church leaders and all that – you had religious people who didn't take to all that [leather]. I understand it was the image they wanted to bring out, but they should have been more tactful." He added: "An MP who was there, Dawn Butler of Brent, said: 'Why are they dressed that way? It doesn't sit right' – and it didn't."

It wasn't just MPs and fellow artists who were indignant either. One mother who didn't want to be named raged that it looked more like the scene of a fetish party than a sombre occasion to commemorate the lives of those lost. "It just wasn't the way I would have wanted my son to be remembered," she explained.

In spite of her fashion faux pas and her struggle to be accepted and taken seriously by urban listeners, it had still been a positive experience for Jessie. Noel believed that she had a stronger voice and more charisma than her girl-band companions, asserting that she was "the one that stood out". While sometimes she'd stood out for all the wrong reasons, it would be what Jessie described as her "golden opportunity" to get noticed.

"They were all bubbly and excited and it was good energy to be around in Soul Deep," Noel remarked. "They were better than the group I was singing with. Their song got most of the promotion and it had the most expensive video, because they were promoting the ones that were strongest." He added: "If it wasn't for Don't Trigger, Jessie might still have got a deal, but it definitely helped – it boosted her confidence and got her hooking up with different people in the entertainment industry."

Indeed, on September 26, the three-track EP was released, attracting a flurry of attention for Jessie from curious music moguls. At one of Soul Deep UK's first ever showcases, she was noticed by a number of record labels scouting for talent.

When she was learning the ropes, it had benefited her to be able to hide behind her more experienced bandmates, while she was developing the confidence and expertise to go it alone. "It was a great time for me to learn about the industry and not be the main one," Jessie confirmed to *YRB* magazine. "To go into a studio but not be the only one that was there." However interest from record labels soon persuaded her it was time to branch out – the girls would no longer act as her comfort blanket.

Flattered by the attention and increasingly feeling that, as a girl group, Soul Deep UK "wasn't going anywhere", Jessie did some quick soul-searching and decided to leave. She'd fulfil her contractual and moral obligations to the campaign, but after that, she'd be battling for a place in the charts solo.

"I had paid my dues," Jessie explained, "and we sat down and I said to the girls: 'I love you guys, but this is what I'm gonna do.' They respected that – and I left."

Chapter 4

A Stroke of Bad Luck

"Sometimes she's a bit wild, but that's Jessie – if you're not wild, you're not a superstar!"

Shae on Jessie J

While several companies were interested in signing Jessie, it was Gut Records – a small but successful independent label – that caught her eye. There was one curveball: some would argue that it had almost zero street cred for serious singers and musicians. For example, the first act ever to be signed, Right Said Fred, had released a novelty single, 'I'm Too Sexy (For My Shirt)', featuring a peacock of a man strutting around boasting that he was so sexy it hurt. His words were delivered with the type of camp affectation that had many listeners hysterical with laughter – great for comedy, but less so for a singer's credibility. To many, it was woefully embarrassing, not to mention a little too camp for the mainstream music lover. Presumably then, no one was more surprised than the Right Said Fred front man himself, when the gimmick went to number one in 28 countries, turning him into an overnight millionaire. The album went on to sell four million copies and the single, described as "criminally catchy", won an Ivor Novello Award for two years running in 1992 and 1993 for Most Played Song.

To its detractors, however, it was merely criminal that it had been allowed to be released. The label, spurred on by its profits with Right Said Fred, went on to acquire entertainers like Tom Jones alongside novelty acts like Mr Blobby, a giant pink cartoon character with huge purple spots, and, in 2005, Crazy Frog, which turned into a worldwide ringtone phenomenon. Back in the nineties, it had also hosted Noel McKoy, who'd worked alongside Jessie on the Don't Trigger campaign, although on the whole, the label was running low on serious acts. Perhaps with Jessie, they could redress the balance.

She was invited to a meeting with the label's boss, Guy Holmes, who'd formerly been head of promotions at Universal, and his colleagues. It was the day of reckoning. The only problem was, she hadn't been entirely truthful in the first meeting. "I went in and they were like, 'Do you write songs?'" Jessie recalled to *I Like Music*. "I was like, 'Yeah, yeah, I write songs all the time!' I was thinking, 'Oh no!' Then [two days later] I wrote my first song."

The label now saw Jessie as a seasoned songwriter. Little did they know that in reality, she hadn't written anything since her attempts at poetry as a nine-year-old. Meanwhile in her teens, her brief lyrical attempts had seen her almost laughed out of the classroom. Plus, she needed more than words to pull off a song – she had to have a competent tune as well.

Terrified that she wouldn't be able to match her bravado when it came to penning her first track, Jessie went into minor meltdown. Should she have owned up and let the label offer her the safe, but boring, option of a pre-written tune? And could her little white lie have cost her the record deal if she couldn't deliver?

The pressure was on, and it was debilitating. She was no longer writing self-indulgent poetry for herself or her friends and it wasn't a hobby any more – it was real. She'd complained bitterly that being in Soul Deep UK had restricted her as she'd been forbidden from writing her own songs. Yet now that she finally had the opportunity to show her stuff lyrically, the nerves were taking hold.

"I remember sitting down in my old house and going: 'Okay, just think like it's a poem with melody,'" she continued. "It was really scary. I think it's the hardest thing to be a songwriter – you can write songs all day every day, but it doesn't mean that anyone wants to listen to them or that they're good."

Jessie was also succumbing to self-doubt as the taunts of her bullies began to echo in her ears, holding her back from achieving her dreams. "I did have people that bullied me and told me I wasn't a good songwriter – and I believed them because I was 15 or 16," she agonised to writer Clayton Perry.

Trying to rise above her insecurities, she thought back to the past, to profound life experiences in her history that she wanted to share with others. One memory that still haunted her was lying opposite a desperately ill boy in Great Ormond Street Hospital at age 11, and watching him pray for his life. "I shared a room with a young boy who was extremely sick and having a heart transplant the following day," she recalled. "That night, I woke up to find the boy out of his bed on the floor praying that God would let him live and he didn't want to die. I listened to him and cried. To my surprise, the young boy passed away the following day. The memory of him praying stuck with me. I didn't quite understand it and I asked my mother: 'Why did he die? He asked God to save him – why didn't God listen?'"

Jessie sat down and began to pour her heart out, and hours later, her anxiety was replaced by a flood of pride. She'd given birth to 'Big White Room'. "It was a big milestone," she told *I Like Music*. "Just because I had written a song and could think, 'I wrote this, this is mine.' I remember singing it to people for the first time and they were like, 'This is really good' and I was like, 'Is it?' It took me a long time to believe in myself as a songwriter."

However, it wasn't to everyone's taste. Just months earlier, The Pussycat Dolls had stormed the charts with the sexually charged 'Don't Cha', an effort which would see the group's debut album *PCD* soar to the top of the US *Billboard* charts. Meanwhile, the previous decade, Jessie's labelmates Right Said Fred had relied on comically audacious boasts about their sex appeal to get ahead.

It was a tried and tested age-old formula for a debut song – sexing up the sound and the image – and Jessie was testing the boundaries by doing the exact opposite. If the music industry was built on sex, drugs and rock'n'roll, The Pussycat Dolls were leading the charge in the first category, Amy Winehouse, Pete Doherty and their crack-pipe cronies took up the second, while countless bands such as The Killers fought for their rights to mainstream notoriety with the third.

Jessie was gate-crashing a world that craved light-hearted entertainment with a pained ballad about a boy who had been seriously ill with a life-threatening heart condition – would it catch on?

Her manager didn't think so – not on paper, at least. "I went to my ex-manager [with the words] and he went, 'That's the tackiest song I've ever heard in my life! Go and change the lyrics!'" Jessie recalled to Clayton Perry. "So I went home. I didn't want to change any lyrics, so I didn't. I went back the next day and sang it to him and he said: 'Amazing! It's a hit!'"

Clearly bucking the trend had paid off. "No one saw that coming," chuckled an anonymous friend. "All of the songs at that time were about dancing in the club or shaking your ass, or 'Baby, I love you!' If it wasn't swagger and sex, it was benign love songs – but Jessie came out with something really deep and intense." She continued: "She was so timid about singing it to anyone at first though. She'd show people the lyrics and go: 'What do you think?' and we'd say: "It would help if we could hear it, Jess!' She had to be persuaded that it sounded just as good out loud as it did in her head."

Showbiz wasn't for the shy and retiring, so, keen to boost her confidence as a songwriter, Raymond sent her to collaborate with a producer known as Shae. He had no shortage of confidence – his personal motto, which he'd jokingly asked Jessie to have tattooed on her inner arm, was: "If the beat ain't fly, the beat ain't mine."

Shae was no stranger to Jessie's voice – he'd had a dramatic first encounter with it in a car park at the video shoot for 'Why?': "There was this coach parked up and I went in, snooping around, when I saw a guy holding his camera up to this girl and she was singing Mariah Carey and Beyoncé," Shae told the author. "I was blown away. I said: 'This girl is sick!'" It was to be the first encounter of many – in fact, the two would go on to become best friends.

After mixing 'Why?', Shae had gone on to write "several albums' worth of material" for Soul Deep UK – but, of course, their debut album was not to be. "Ray said: 'I'm not sure if you know, but Jessie wants to go solo and I want you to create a song for her,'" Shae recalled.

Jessie had grown desperately unhappy with the catfights over designer clothes and the battles about who'd be centre stage, but – without even knowing of the group's politics – Shae hadn't been surprised to learn that Jessie was going solo. "Being in a group is like a family - if you don't bicker, there's something wrong!" he joked. "[But] you could tell Jessie was a lead singer. She's like Nicole Scherzinger in The Pussycat Dolls – you know she's the one who's gonna be in the forefront, regardless. She stood out. She's a very strong-minded person and was always going to be a solo artist. There could never be a group to launch her – it had to be her coming out on her own."

Jessie was like Beyoncé, too. Destiny's Child had survived a couple of line-up changes but, no matter who came and went, Beyoncé was always a constant – and was unwaveringly the centre of attention. She'd seemed green-lit for a solo career from the beginning.

What was more, once she'd made it on her own, she wasted no time in unleashing her inner sexy diva. Gone was the braided hair and the demure trouser suits – Beyoncé was flashing the flesh with reckless abandon. There were glittery leotards and tight lycra dresses. Beyoncé was setting out to show that her curves were just as voluptuous as her voice.

She'd gone from the woman who'd berated other girls for being "sleazy" with their clothes to becoming a self-proclaimed "naughty girl", shaking her hips in the jungle while singing about cavorting with Sean Paul and then dirty dancing with Jay-Z. She'd gone from someone who'd sworn she'd never kiss a girl as it would compromise her Christian values to one who'd acted out an entire implied lesbian love story with Lady Gaga in the video for 'Telephone'. At heart, Beyoncé still seemed to be a conservative girl, but on stage she'd let out the alter ego she called Sasha Fierce – and where was the harm in that? It now seemed Jessie was about to make the same transformation.

"In the beginning stages, I gave her swagger," Shae revealed. "It came from myself and [my production team], Feng Shui. We gave her the street sense. She had her own style, but we gave her that oomph to come out of her shell, which I think she wanted to do anyway. She was a normal Essex girl before, not chavvy, but she was plain. Soul Deep wasn't an in-your-face star-studded group – they wore earthy colours and were very emotional – but that's what Soul Deep was about. However, I don't think that's what she wanted. They were all pretty girls with all different nationalities – like a Neapolitan ice cream, with different flavours for everyone – but Jessie wanted something different."

Underneath the mousy brown fringe, Jessie had a secret appetite for something sexier – a look that was as loud as her voice. She might have been "prim and proper" in Soul Deep UK, but things were about to change drastically.

According to Shae, prising Jessie out of the type of leather outfit she'd worn at the Don't Trigger showcase would be like "trying to get Pete Doherty to stop taking heroin – impossible!"

Indeed, even 25 court appearances and 15 drugs charges weren't enough to convince Pete to break his addiction – a little thing like braving a solo career wasn't about to stop Jessie from indulging hers.

Jessie was also interested in experimenting with her sound. She wanted to be different and Shae was already different – they were the perfect match. In a bid to get her started, Shae's mission was to wean her off her beloved soul divas, removing the vocal acrobatics of Mariah Carey and Whitney Houston and replacing them with a tougher, more street sound. He lent Jessie his favourite CDs – Missy Elliott, Jay-Z and Timbaland.

She'd also been in the studio with Amplify Dot, a determined artist two years her senior and one of Shae's closest friends, who'd been invited on stage with Missy Elliott at age 14. Missy had predicted she'd be a big hit, so if hip hop was the direction Jessie wanted to follow, she was confident she was in the right hands.

However, it wasn't plain sailing. Shae was a trendsetter rather than a follower and he knew he was taking a risk by launching her into a genre that, back in the mid 2000s, wasn't getting much mainstream radio play. But, surrounded by a wealth of female artists who were already signed, Jessie knew she had to stand out from the crowd.

"At the time when we were doing it, it was very underground," Shae revealed. "There was a small market for it here in the UK and it wasn't very commercial at all. Back then, the only time you'd hear black music was from America. In later years, a lot of black urban artists were introduced, mixed with a European house sound, but at the time we were doing it, we were getting no love."

He added: "It was on a Channel U level – we were getting no respect. We wanted to do an American approach but from the UK, something commercially viable but still underground. We were looking for a sound at a time when female singers were rife. They were everywhere, the Amys, the Adeles – if you're going to get signed, you need to be different. Raymond had a vision [for her] and we had to home in on that and get it right."

The pressure was on. Shae even experimented with developing her as a rapper and had aspirations of himself and his Feng Shui colleague Fontz becoming the UK version of The Black Eyed Peas with Jessie as their front woman. "This was in the days before N-Dubz became famous but me, Fontz and Jessie would have been like Tulisa, Dappy and Fazer!" Shae enthused. "We'd write Missy Elliott-orientated, abstract songs that could be played in the club. We'd talk about how much we loved Adidas, how fly we are, how we're better than everyone else – it was very clubby, very boastful."

That was the flavour of their first hip-hop song, 'Like That', which Shae described as a "very, very hard unreleased club track". It was a big step for a girl who'd grown up with Mariah Carey's love songs playing on repeat – but, fortunately for Shae, she learned fast and was determined to embody their vibe. "I educated her on the hip-hop side and just gave her a little bit of a hint," Shae recalled. "She wanted to be funky, but just needed that little catalyst."

What was more, Jessie was still self-disciplined, working daily on the quality of her voice. "It's like being a body-builder – you need to build up the muscle," Shae continued. "I've met a lot of singers blessed by God with great vocals but they don't want to work on it. Your voice is an instrument – you HAVE to put work in."

He added: "Jessie was also a very intelligent girl. She's like a sponge, she will absorb anything that's around her. She'd see someone wearing multicoloured Adidas high-top trainers and she won't get the same pair but will take the idea and make it her own. Sometimes she's a bit wild – but that's Jessie."

The ingredients were there, but as yet they hadn't quite perfected the product – and Jessie still didn't have the record deal she craved. Gut was keen, but the deal-maker was to deliver a song that would fit as her first single. That song was 'Catwalk'.

"I came up with the idea of a quirky, funky, soulful song with swagger – Jessie always had the voice but didn't have the swagger at that time – and I went home and created 'Catwalk'," Shae recalled. "It was the song that would get her signed. It was very funk orientated, that bass sound – think James Brown on crack, that kinda vibe. It was also inspired by some sixties Motown sounds and a lot of old-school jazz."

Jessie's stance was fiercely anti-drugs – with a heart condition, one innocent experiment would kill her. She'd once berated Shae for merely drinking a can of beer in her presence – but she was in luck during the making of the song, as the hardest drug he was on was chocolate. It might have sounded like James Brown on crack, but Shae was just on a sugar high. That inspired him to write the anthem about non-conformity.

"'Catwalk' was about not conforming to the way the world is. Instead of wearing high heels and size zero clothes and stuff, it was about high-top trainers, baggy jeans and funky stuff. You're on the catwalk but you're louder than everyone else and crazily dressed," Shae explained. "You've got the standard couture stuff and then you come out with all your stuff and you look better than everyone else!"

Like Beyoncé's 'Get Me Bodied', there were constant references to the supermodel Naomi Campbell in the chorus – the diva both artists had been channelling. However the boastful vibe of a woman strutting her stuff on the catwalk and feeling fine was in fact inspired by the musical threesome of Nelly Furtado, Justin Timberlake and Timbaland on their song 'Give It To Me'. On the tune, Nelly sings that she is a supermodel.

A bit of boastful bravado was nothing new in the music business, but did Jessie have what it took? Rapper Drake might have bragged that his first name was "greatest" and his last name was "ever" on the song 'Forever', but that same tune was an effort that had sold over 1 million downloads and pushed its way to the top of America's rap charts. He had a reason to rate himself, no matter how brash it might have sounded.

Meanwhile, the ever modest Kanye West regarded himself as a "superhero", an "icon", a "fashion reference" and – whenever he ran out of superlatives – simply "the best". He'd told the press: "I realise that my place and position in history is that I will go down as the voice of this generation, of this decade – I will be the loudest voice!" and, "I am the tree and the people are the branches."

What was more, googling the term "Kanye West's arrogance" returns well over 1 million hits. Still, it wasn't just arrogance he was good at – he also had a great success rate with selling CDs. His last four albums each made number one in America, where he also sold over 25 million digital downloads – and he had won a record-breaking total of 14 Grammy Awards. Even the star's father, Ray, had publicly admonished his son in *Rolling Stone* magazine, claiming: "That's not how you were raised." Yet Kanye's last words on the matter? "I still believe that I am the greatest."

Then there was the queen of bravado, Beyoncé, with the inflatable ego that had earned its own song in honour of it. Yet tellingly, the lyrics of 'Ego' boast that she can back it up. Indeed, all four of her albums had debuted at number one in the US charts and she'd sold in excess of 75 million CDs worldwide. While she'd steered clear of any self-adoration that matched Kanye West's proportions, she'd not been shy about praising herself, because she had the worldwide chart domination to prove her claims.

However, Jessie hadn't – was such a level of shameless arrogance advisable for someone who, as yet, hadn't even bagged themselves a record deal? It turned out that it was, as 'Catwalk' was all the convincing Gut Records needed to sign her up. Jessie finally had her first solo deal.

To Shae, they had found the perfect sound – they now needed to work on stepping up her image to match her vocals. "She was very plain Jane," he observed. "You need to be a star and stand out in everything you do." However, the pair's work on revitalising her image was cut out when Jessie's song became a prophecy and she was approached by a real life model scout.

"When I was 17, I was shopping with my sister in Oxford Street and I got stopped by this lady and she said: 'Do you want to be a hair model?'" Jessie recalled to VEVO. "I kinda wanted to do something with my hair but hadn't really decided, so she took me into Vidal Sassoon and she was like: 'We're going to cut it asymmetrical, with a fringe' and I was like: 'Okay, this could be pretty cool' and I came out looking like something out of *Star Trek!*"

Things were even worse in the cold light of morning. "The funniest thing I remember is getting up the next day and trying to do it myself and [it] looking more like a mushroom than a haircut!" she joked. She had cringed with embarrassment when giant adverts with her face on them were emblazoned across bus windows in an array of ludicrous styles. She went through mullets, mohawks and finally the jet-black, poker-straight bob with a fringe that would become her trademark look. For better or worse, Jessie had become the face of Vidal Sassoon.

It might have been embarrassing, but it was also lucrative – for a cash-strapped student like Jessie, whose life was consumed by auditioning, practising and performing, she needed to step up financially so she could continue with her vocal tuition. "I had the most ridiculous haircuts," she told Clayton Perry, "but I always said to myself: 'You know what? I look like I'm flying on *Star Trek*, but it's paying for my singing lessons!'"

Years later, Jessie would tell *The Independent* she'd "had the same haircut since I was five" – but she hadn't quite been telling the truth. In fact, her styles would become so out-there that it encouraged her friends to experiment with their own looks. "I was always the friend that people would say: 'Oh, I can wear something different because I'm going out with Jessie. I can get away with it because I'm with her!'" she later told *Bliss*. She added: "Going to school was never the same again – I was always the girl with the crazy hair!"

One thing was for sure – she certainly wouldn't be fielding any more accusations that she was a "plain Jane". Her work with Vidal Sassoon made Jessie a little more daring about her own style experiments too. Not only did she once dye her hair "15 different colours" to "express myself", she would also adorn her face with music notes to prove her dedication to her trade. It might not have stood out much in a classroom full of extroverted attention seekers at the BRIT School, but it did attract a lot of curiosity elsewhere.

While she might not have taken things as far as permanent tattoos, she was determined to show her star quality on the outside. She was taking the message of 'Catwalk' to heart – she'd watched every episode of *America's Next Top Model*, idolised judge Tyra Banks and had tried to perfect her walk and smile. "I watched every series and I learned a lot from her," Jessie told VEVO. "It was all about smizing – smiling with your eyes!"

At 5ft 9in, Jessie had the height of an aspiring model. Thanks to her style lessons with Shae, she wasn't short on swagger either. However, the girl formerly so healthy that she'd been forbidden from eating at McDonald's now had one weakness – snacking on sugary sweets in the studio.

Sugar, described by one popular self-help book as "the white death", is not only fattening but potentially harmful. Containing neither vitamins nor minerals, it draws from the body's own reserve of nutrients in order to be metabolised into the system, depleting the nutritional value of any other food that has been eaten. The eater then craves more and more sugar to sustain energy levels – and the cravings begin. Not only that, but too much sugar could have an ageing effect equivalent to the drinking and smoking that Jessie detested. Nutritionist Alex Manos revealed: "Once refined sugar enters the bloodstream, it attaches to proteins to form harmful new molecules [which] damage any adjacent proteins… Proteins found in the skin such as collagen and elastin become damaged, contributing to the appearance of dry skin, wrinkles and sagging."

Terrified by the prospect of wrinkles and cellulite so young, a 17-year-old Jessie embarked on a detox diet, supplementing sugary snacks with juice drinks and raw foods as part of her anti-sugar health plan. However, it would have disastrous consequences. "I was snacking on so much sugary stuff that all the nutrients in my food weren't being absorbed, so I was given all these drinks to have every day and I was only allowed raw food, to flush my system out," Jessie recalled to MTV. "I went for days and oh, it was bad. I was going to a gig with my dad and I said to him: 'I need to poo myself!' I had to rush to someone's house and I won't even tell you what happened." The ever honest Jessie then had a change of heart, confessing: "It's the most embarrassing thing that ever happened to me and I was 17. It's not like I was four – I was an adult!"

Meanwhile, her life was about to get even less glamorous when she signed up for a part-time job in central London's Hamleys toy store. Jessie might have had a record deal, but that was where the hard work truly began. Far from a life of champagne dinners and showbiz parties, in between frantic recording sessions and lessons at the BRIT School, she found herself trying to make ends meet by giving "spoiled children" nail-art demonstrations.

Her only audience now was the throngs of screaming preteens that would descend on the store and the best melody would be their indignant bellows and high-pitched squeals when they were denied one of the season's latest must-haves. Even more demanding than a socialite in a Gucci store, and even more hysterical than a woman on a strict diet passing by a sweet shop, these children were not for the faint hearted. "You would get these crazy kids that would throw tantrums because they'd literally had like 18 gobstoppers and they'd be like: 'I just want a pencil – I just want something!'" Jessie recalled to MTV.

First would come begging, pleading and cajoling – and then, when that failed, they would be reduced to full-throttle tantrums on the shop floor. Through all weathers, Jessie kept "smizing". Her acting background helped her to keep a cheerful face. "I did 'nail jazz' so I was basically drawing snowmen, Christmas trees and smiley faces," she continued. "I used to lose my voice all the time, because I'd be like, 'HELLO! Would you like a nail-jazz demonstration?'"

Sore throats from enthusiastic sales pitches and headaches from hyperactive children weren't the only hazards of the job though – and Jessie soon found herself with a crippling hand injury. "I was hardcore, I actually gave myself a thumb injury!" she laughed. "I had a specific muscle that I actually ripped from doing so many [nails] every day." While the job was draining, at least she was able to add nail art to her list of talents. "The positive of the job was that now I can draw a snowman or a Christmas tree on anyone's nails!" she added.

On top of her hair modelling, nail art and studio sessions, Jessie also had a job on a fruit and nut confectionery stall at an Essex market. By this point, she had four jobs at once and, even though she'd clinched a record deal, she hadn't let the singing lessons slide either.

By day, she would divide her time between the BRIT School – where she barely missed a lesson – and the studio, while by night she would attend gigs with her producers, sometimes taking to the stage herself. Jessie's working life seemed busy enough to rival the average investment banker at times, so perhaps it was little wonder that occasionally she didn't put in the practise needed.

One day, fresh from the hip-hop styles of the studio in Brixton, she arrived at BRIT unprepared for her scheduled performance of a classical musical theatre tune – the polar opposite of what she'd just been doing.

"We had to rehearse for a revue show based on the work of Maltby and Shire," classmate Aisha Ludmilla recalled to the author. "I remember our teachers pairing us up to sing a duet on the song 'Back To Base' [from the musical *Closer Than Ever*] and I also remember being very nervous because everyone knew she had an awesome voice. I was quite scared! [But] when it came to the performance, she told me she was unable to sing it with me [as she hadn't learned it]. But before I went up to perform it, she gave me some tips and encouragement, which I was very thankful for. At first I was quite intimidated by her, but then I realised she was quite down to earth, a hard worker who was well grounded."

Jessie was back on form for her final year performance where she took the lead role in popular play *Sweet Charity*. An award-winning musical, it had been a favourite on Broadway and in the West End since 1966.

Charity is an unlikely dancehall hostess and implied prostitute who, in spite of her slightly seedy profession, is a hopeless romantic who dreams of love and marriage. Unlike the hardened fellow hostesses she works beside, who have hearts of steel and suits of armour to protect their emotions, she is continually getting hurt by a string of unsuitable men. One of her co-workers tells her she runs her heart like a hotel, allowing a constant stream of people to check in and out.

Big-hearted but small-brained, she gives her hard-earned cash to beggars until she has none left for herself. Even worse, while she romanticises about a happy marriage with her boyfriend, he is plotting to steal her wallet, pushing her into a lake before making off with her handbag.

Men treat her with disrespect, disregarding her feelings and dismissing her as just another working girl. Charity is less streetwise and, instead of playing them at their own game and trying to get what she can from her faux suitors, she always falls in love and gets her heart broken. Her luck seems to change when she meets a big-screen celebrity, Vidal, and is seduced by him – only to be humiliated when his mistress returns following a fight and she is forced to watch their lovemaking through a crack in the door of the wardrobe she hides in.

A mortified Charity is smuggled out of the house the next day without so much as a goodbye, while her fellow dancers berate her for not making any money from the encounter. Downtrodden and disrespected, she ends up stuck in an elevator – a metaphor for the rut her life is in – when she finally meets a good man, who knows nothing about her profession and the double life she leads.

At first insisting she is a bank clerk, she finds the courage to tell him the truth later and, after quitting her job, plans their marriage. Ultimately, however, her former work is too much for the man who could have made her happy – and yet again she finds herself pushed into the lake. The musical ends with Charity living not happily, but hopefully, ever after.

The role of Charity was triple-cast, meaning that Jessie and her classmates Michaela and Ria alternated between being the star attraction and minor roles as extras. Jessie, however, was determined to be the centre of attention every night.

"Ria had the last night but Jessie was trying to steal the limelight by overacting and singing really loud," Kerry Louise Barnaby recalled to the author. "With her background singing, she was trying to upstage her and making everything over the top so you just had to watch her."

Aisha Ludmilla had similar memories, chuckling: "In the train scene, Jessie and I were extras. While Charity was given her line, Jessica, who was playing an old woman, was making the funniest faces and as a result nobody was even paying any attention to the lead!"

The train scene had been a real cliff-hanger moment, when a besotted Oscar – the man Charity had met in an elevator – asks what she does for a living. However, thanks to Jessie's face-pulling antics, the entire audience were watching an elderly woman sitting silently in the corner of the carriage.

The show would be Jessie's parting shot. She'd earned top marks in her practical work, which she'd combined with A-level subjects such as sociology, an interest due to her father's profession. She then left the BRIT School with a performance at the leaving ceremony, when – once again – all eyes were on her. "I wore this awful red dress and I had a Lego Man haircut," Jessie shuddered to *Elle Girl* of the evening. "I won a sociology award and I was predicted an A, but when I got my results back I got a D, which wasn't so good – but at least I got to perform."

According to Aisha Ludmilla, that was all she'd wanted. "I know there are people who come to the BRIT School just simply to get the qualification and get any job remotely connected to what they had studied," she claimed. "Not Jessica! I could tell that it was her main goal in life to be a recording artist. She had the whole package – looks, personality and – most importantly – the talent."

Graduating from the BRIT School gave Jessie the opportunity to spend more time with new-found producer friends like Shae and Amplify Dot as well as a female singer called Kira, who would go on to become her lover, and an MC known as Roxanne.

"Me, Jessie and A-Dot were best friends," Shae revealed to the author. "We'd catch the most jokes and we'd go out and have fun times. We had some stupid fucking jokes, very childish – Jessie used to call me Moon Man and we had a lot of private jokes that nobody else would understand. Everyone would be like, 'Why are you doing that?' Nobody would understand but we would think it was hilarious. We'd put a bottle on the floor and go, 'Hello, bottle!' This was without smoking anything – we were mad even without intoxication."

That was just as well as – despite Jessie and her friends' constant presence on the Brixton and West End club scene – she had a zero tolerance policy on alcohol. "She used to hate drinking," Shae added. "She used to get high on Red Bull [instead]. She'd be like: 'Why are you drinking?' Sue me. It's a Marmite thing and that's what she had with alcohol."

When the pair weren't clubbing, they would go on trips to theme parks such as Alton Towers, or Jessie would "watch intently" while Shae produced and mixed her tracks in the studio. Some were co-written, while at times they would create songs separately. According to Shae, they were "the tightest of friends" – and they would go on to produce more than 100 tracks together.

Gut Records had already given the green light to 'Catwalk' as Jessie's first single and she and Shae were in the process of whittling down their other songs to select the best ones to accompany the track on her album when their attention was distracted by a new project. Raymond was planning another year of promotion for the Don't Trigger campaign – and he wanted Jessie to get involved.

The 2005 campaign had been just a three-track EP, but now there were plans for a full-length album. One of the main tracks was 'A Mother's Ballad', which Shae had produced months earlier without the campaign in mind – but Ray had fallen in love with it. "I was sitting there in a very R&B slow jam kind of mood," Shae recalled. "I used a sample of a road sound from Missy Elliott's album. Ray wanted me to do the whole soundtrack for the Don't Trigger album and I played this track to him and he goes: 'Ahh, I need that!'"

Hil St. Soul was invited in to write the song based on Shae's beat – a two piece consisting of Zambian singer and songwriter Hilary Mwelwa and her producer Victor Redwood-Sawyerr. Grenada-born singer Juliet Roberts, who'd enjoyed several Top 20 UK hits, also lent her voice, while the third singer in the trio was Jocelyn Brown, whose 1986 track 'Love's Gonna Get You' was a worldwide hit. The lyric "I've got the power" was sampled by the group Snap for their song 'The Power', which was synonymous with action TV show *Gladiators*.

The three had been scheduled to record the song alone. Adding Jessie's voice to the mix had been a mere afterthought, but – to some – she stole the show, outshining the more seasoned divas entirely. "We had three big divas on the track and then we said: 'Why not put Jessie on it?'" Shae recalled, "and no disrespect to the divas, but Jessie killed it. She held her own – and these are big divas, big women I've listened to since I was a child. I heard her and I was like:'How does she do that? She's sick!'The others were great. It was like: 'Do you know who that is? That's Juliet Roberts right there!' but I preferred Jessie."

His opinion was controversial. Hilary Mwelwa had voiced some of her beliefs the same year about favouritism and racism in the music industry, berating those in charge for giving extra attention to white artists. She felt that black soul singers were left in the background and frequently overshadowed by their more marketable white counterparts. Speaking to black culture magazine *Essence*, she blasted: "I'm noticing that people like the Amy Winehouses and the Adeles get a bigger push from labels. There are not that many black female artists actually getting signed in the UK. It really is about the Adeles, Duffys and Amys. It does have a negative impact and you question it. A black female artist singing soul music versus a white artist singing soul or whatever you want to call it, we don't seem to get the same kind of love that they do."

Some might agree that the mainstream music lover in Britain was white and therefore might identify more with a blonde Caucasian singer like Duffy, for example.Were black singers being marginalised and treated unfairly? Did Hilary feel that Jessie, who stood out like a sore thumb as a pale-skinned oddity in the middle of a group of three black women, was just a talentless spare part, there purely to draw attention from white audiences? Hilary went on to tell *Essence*:"It's not to say that I don't feel Amy Winehouse deserves to have that spotlight on her, but everybody should get the same opportunity and I don't think the UK's black female artists do."

Some Anglo-American black women had also joined the debate, contesting that soul music had originated from black America and that it belonged to them. Jessie had found herself drawn into yet another implicit race dispute just by her presence on the song – but, fortunately for her, most people were focused purely on the campaign's message.

"At the time it wasn't about Jessie," Shae confirmed. "All she cared about at that time was getting the message across. That track was emotional. Jessie was actually crying at the video shoot. I spent eight months on the album and ended up in hospital with exhaustion and she phoned me up at the shoot and told me. In the video you could see that she had tears in her eyes."

This claim would counter the beliefs of some that Jessie had been unemotional and detached from the campaign due to gun crime being so far removed from her everyday life.

She also starred as a solo act in the song 'A Long Goodbye' where she channelled a woman caught up in a violent relationship who ended her life paralysed by a knife wound to the neck. Did Jessie have urban street cred? The Don't Trigger website seemed to think so, praising: "Once in a while you come across an artist that will leave you breathless and questioning why some of us are born with unparalleled ability and some of us spend endless years striving and failing to achieve it. Jessie J has all the qualities needed to reach the top and more. Not only is her vocal ability unquestionable, but her commitment and conviction to her art form is unrivalled."

Not only did Jessie have the full support of her management on Don't Trigger, but the word was also being spread by getting Jessie out on the touring circuit and into the public eye ahead of her first single.

"She did a showcase at [London club] Café de Paris and at places like Ramshackle Chelsea," Shae recalled. "Whenever there was an opportunity, she was out there, but Raymond always made sure it was his event or a prestigious event and made sure it was well placed and that industry people were there."

She'd also do freestyle sessions at Patrick Allan's night The Music Box, held at the Pigalle Club in London's West End. "If Patrick knows you're talented, he'll just bring you up on the stage!" Shae explained.

Open-mic nights weren't Jessie's only opportunity to shine, either. Gut also sent her out on the road as an unknown support act for established artists such as Taio Cruz, The Sugababes, Jools Holland and Macy Gray. It was a challenge, but one that would get her used to the touring circuit and ease her in gently.

"They all had totally different audiences," Jessie recalled to *I Like Music*. "For Jools Holland, we had to strip our stuff down to just me and Ben [Martinez, her then guitarist]. With Macy Gray, it was a PA and two backing vocalists and it was totally different. It taught me so much about myself – to be able to adapt to different audiences, different types of music, to cater to such a vast audience, a global kind of sound."

What was more, this was Jessie's chance to build up confidence and expertise while the limelight was positioned safely away from her and focused on the main attraction. Nobody would notice the mistakes she made and she could move up from amateur to established performer without anyone there to document her mistakes.

"I'm glad I had to learn how to be amazing on stage like that, how to fill somewhere the size of Wembley Arena with no press, no features, no record, no band behind me," Jessie told *YRB*. "It toughens you up. Being on stage is my home. Even if it's 20 minutes, I'll take control of it because that is my time. It's when I come to life. It's just me, my heels and my mic."

Jessie might have enjoyed the anonymity, but – to her surprise – when she supported Macy Gray at London's O2 Arena, all eyes were on her. "That was when she started to get a lot of recognition," Shae recalled. "Jessie was the fucking support act, but she blew the place up and, when she finished, the place was empty. The crowd was patchy!"

Whether it was jamming with her hip-hop friends at understated freestyle nights, or playing ballads with international stars on arena tours, Jessie was pulling a diverse audience – and instead of impatiently craving the headliner, they were starting to listen.

By this time, she was almost ready to launch her album. More than 150 songs had been written and, while some were fit to "hit the iTunes garbage bin", she still had plenty of credible material to fill an album. She'd also found her trademark style, combining the edgy, urban street sound she'd been trying to perfect with some soulful Lauryn Hill-style singing. "*The Miseducation Of Lauryn Hill* is the best album I've ever heard," she revealed later to *I Like Music*. "It was one of the first albums that made me want to write songs. It was so autobiographical and that's exactly how I am as a writer. I just listened to it and I thought, 'This is so honest', and the way it was put together was so educational but not preachy. It was just very inspirational. I hope my album can give to young people the same thing that her album did."

Lauryn Hill had stuck out like a sore thumb when she'd first arrived on the music scene. She'd broken into what was then a white world, defiantly touting a black American accent and braids and combining rap with ballad-like vocals. What was more, in a world of free love where sex sold and many female singers made their music memorable by writhing in front of the camera in skimpy costumes, Lauryn was deliberately different. Her music spoke of dignity, self-respect, monogamy, not giving away your body, avoiding revealing clothes and even reading the Bible. She couldn't have been more different from the average pop artist – and yet her music was selling fast. That was what Jessie wanted to achieve – commercial success on her own terms and for being herself, no matter how counter-cultural she seemed to be.

Lauryn had spoken passionately about addictive relationships where neither party could let go, had talked frankly about the bad side of life just as much as the good side and had offered songs from the heart rather than from a manufactured script. That too was the result Jessie was looking for – and she believed in it so much, Katy B had even spotted her that year doing a tribute to Lauryn in a Croydon nightclub.

Jessie was ready for lift-off. Gut believed in her, the producers believed in her and her family and friends were right behind her too. The day of reckoning was about to arrive, but before her new single could so much as hit the charts, disaster struck.

One moment Jessie had been working on her music and the next she woke up in hospital, paralysed. It was the type of twist of fate that nightmares were made of – at just 19, she had had a stroke.

Chapter 5

Perfectly Flawed

"Boo as much as you want – but I'll boo back!"

Jessie J

Jessie couldn't have just had a stroke. That was what happened to elderly people with high blood pressure and a junk-food diet – wasn't it? Painfully for her, Jessie was living proof that even outwardly healthy teenage girls were susceptible.

She'd been in Hamleys practising her nail-art sales pitch one weekend when she collapsed, losing the feeling in her right side altogether. The first question on Jessie's mind as she was rushed to hospital was: "Why?"

"I was sat in the hospital, thinking: 'Woah, hold up a minute, why did I have a stroke?'" Jessie revealed to *Glamour.* "It made me realise that, whoever you are, wherever you're from, however many times you run or whatever you do eat or don't eat, shit happens and you get ill."

Jessie's nightmare unfolded even further when doctors broke it to her that her paralysis might be permanent – and there was a chance that she would never be able to walk or sing again.

Perhaps she'd been living her life in the fast lane for too long – after all, she'd had four jobs. She'd been an Essex market-stall trader, an international hair model, a nail-bar girl and smiling saleswoman with nerves of steel all in one – and a fearless support-act singer all around the country. To top that off, Jessie had barely missed a day at the BRIT School.

A classmate revealed to the author: "To say Jessie was dedicated was an understatement. All the other girls would skip classes because they were hungover or busy with their social lives, but in two years I don't remember her missing a single lesson. She took a few days off for a heart problem but that was it. Actually, from her attitude, you'd never have thought she was battling with anything at all."

As she'd had an exemplary lifestyle, an immaculate diet and had avoided alcohol and drugs, stress stood out as the main culprit. The demands of dozens of screaming children clamouring for toys and wriggling in her lap as she painted novelty symbols on their nails might have seemed an obvious catalyst. For those who didn't take to children or favoured a quiet life, it was the job from hell. But had the ear-splitting screams of – irritating but innocent really – preteen children really been the recipe for her downfall?

Jessie's anonymous classmate had another theory – that it was accumulated stress from her days of being in a girl group. "Jessie's a really gentle girl and she was never involved in any viciousness or bickering," she explained. "She doesn't let haters into her head space. But she was dealing with some massive egos in that band. It might have been better if they'd already made it, but at that stage each girl was a potential rival for the others."

She added: "They were all trying to hit the big time and didn't want to be overshadowed, even by each other. Even small things like who would get to wear the show-stopper dress or who would get more camera time in future videos was potentially a reason for argument. Jessie didn't care as much about the little things, but they were all fighting among themselves to be the front woman of the group."

According to her, it was this infighting that had sabotaged their chances of making it to the top, too. "You have to be a unit," she claimed. "It's difficult. How can you field the jealousy and criticism from the haters on the outside when that kind of thing is going on within the band too? Those girls were their own worst enemies – and yes, there was crying

Not your average pop star – Jessie J dons a Lolita-like Minnie Mouse bow together with an incongruent T-shirt honouring hard rock group Deep Purple to promote her debut album. DAVE HOGAN/GETTY IMAGES

A virtually unrecognisable 15-year-old Jessie poses with her proud parents after winning the Best Young Pop Singer category on ITV show *Britain's Brilliant Prodigies* in 2003. ITV/REX FEATURES

Before the jet black bob and the costumes: Jessie poses with Robin Gibb of the Bee Gees, who presented her award on the night. ITV/REX FEATURES

Jessie's best weapon is her mouth – and she's got a microphone! This early win was a sign of things to come. ITV/REX FEATURES

Jessie's miniature identical twin from the 'Who's Laughing Now' video is a serious contender for her swagger on stage at the V Festival in Chelmsford, on August 20, 2011. JAMES MCCAULEY/REX FEATURES

Jessie poses in Berlin shortly after her win at the 2011 BRIT Awards. BRITTA PEDERSEN/DPA/CORBIS and drama, I think. Don't get me wrong, they were friends at heart and there were no handbags at dawn. They did stay friends up to the day they split and probably beyond, but it was never easy."

A final major divide between Jessie and her three rivals was alcohol. It had been something that had also set her apart from her friends at the BRIT School. "People were intimidated by Jessie because she seemed so self-assured and was such a great singer," her classmate continued. "They found it hard to trust her and relax around her if they were drinking and she was sober. It was the same in the band; they were young girls and they liked to party, but that was never Jessie's scene."

Alcohol wasn't just an almost obligatory social lubricant. For many teenagers, it was even more important than showbiz when would-be starlets all too often found themselves drinking to calm their nerves before each show. Yet for Jessie, even succumbing to a few glasses of wine for Dutch courage wasn't possible. "I've had to base my confidence on purity," she had told the BBC of the heart problem that had forced her to abstain. "I can't go onstage with a double G&T or a spliff in my body. I have to go onstage as me, because I can't do any of that stuff."

The drinking culture both in the industry and within Soul Deep UK was rife and Jessie began to feel increasingly alienated. "I won't say she grew apart from the other Soul Deep girls because they were never really together," her classmate added. "These girls wanted to bag a famous boyfriend and be the Jay-Z and Beyoncé of showbiz so they were always on the party circuit, surrounded by booze and boys, and then there was Jessie – the teetotal lesbian. She didn't fit in."

While Jessie had dated men, she was beginning to feel more comfortable with herself, enough to start to admit that it was girls she preferred.

She and the other band members were friendly but were never going to be bosom buddies and they'd never be able to share the experience of losing control after a night of binge drinking. However, was her awkward relationship with the other three really a recipe so ill-fated that it had led to her stroke? Her classmate seemed to think so, laughing off the suggestion that a life of working in Hamleys had been the final straw. "Being in a girl group definitely put her on the fast track to getting a stroke – the stress was like nothing else she'd ever known," she claimed.

Whatever had caused the problem, Jessie now found her dreams thwarted as she lay in hospital, knowing that the odds were against her. Statistically, the majority of stroke victims never regain full functioning of their bodies afterwards. Seething with frustration, she began the waiting game, feeling weak, exhausted and numb. "You know when people go: 'You're 18 and you've got all the time in the world?'" she later raged to the BBC. "I was, like, 'Well, no, I've just had a stroke and I don't think I do.'"

Fortunately, she slowly regained the sensation in her side. However, it was a wake-up call, prompting her to throw herself into pursuing her dream. "I've looked at the big stuff straight in the eye, had people sitting on the end of a hospital bed wondering what's going to happen next and genuinely not knowing," she told the *Evening Standard*. "[My stroke] definitely gave me an insight in that however healthy I am, however well I was brought up – cuz I never had junk food, I never smoked, I never drank alcohol – sometimes health isn't something that is on your side. You can either embrace that, get over it and go: 'Okay, cool, I still got my sight, I can hear, I can walk, I can breathe, I can see' or give up."

That was one thing that was never an option for Jessie, who seemed to tread the fine line between determination and masochism. She'd practised dancing en pointe without so much as a grimace of discomfort and even carrying a heart monitor hadn't deterred her from succeeding in her classes. Like her parents, Jessie was a "go-getter" and – instead of discouraging her – adversity was only going to spur her on.

"It's one of those things that makes you think: 'Okay, life isn't guaranteed for anybody, so it's time for me to turn this on and really do it justice," she told the BBC. "I can look back on it now and go: 'You know what? I'm glad I went through the tough times and was angry.' It's made me a thicker-skinned artist and I think you have to be tough."

Rather than becoming a sob story – someone who was pitied instead of admired – she used her bad health to demonstrate that it was possible to succeed against all odds. "I don't want my health to define me," she revealed. "Yes, I have bad health issues, but it could be a lot worse. I don't want it to be my boo-hoo story. I almost want it to be the opposite.

I wanna be a role model for anyone who has disabilities or health issues that doesn't feel like they can live their dream, because it's complete and utter lies."

Jessie left hospital and returned home with a renewed desire to succeed. The fear of losing the talent she loved the most had propelled her into action. Singing was no longer a whimsical ambition, shelved away on a to-do list for the future – it was now or never.

"I kicked into gear and didn't take any shit from anyone," Jessie recalled to *Glamour*. "When you're sitting there thinking: 'Will I walk again? Will I sing again? Will my right side go back to normal?', you think: 'I haven't got time to waste!' I said to the record company: 'This is what my album's going to sound like and you're going to stop trying to put me into a bikini next to a rapper!'"

Unfortunately she was a little late in making that revelation – Gut Records had just gone bankrupt. "I had an album ready to go – mixed, mastered, a single, a massive media campaign [on the way] – and then they went bankrupt!" Jessie agonised to Neon Limelight. "That's when I was left kinda going: 'Oh no!'"

The financial affairs of the company had been crumbling fast – in just a year, the money in the bank had dwindled from almost half a million pounds down to just £12,000 – and their debts were soaring, leaving them with no choice but to bow out at a loss. By August 2008, Gut had gone into administration.

The company's founder, Guy Holmes, would emerge victorious when he was invited to play a leading role in raising new record label Two Seas – launched by the Prince of Bahrain – which would have released Michael Jackson's comeback album and autobiography. Guy also began to pursue interests in Formula 1 racing – but what about Jessie? It was maddening to have the plug pulled on her at such a critical time.

Perhaps, however, it was a blessing in disguise. Gut had a track record of recruiting less than serious acts such as Right Said Fred, which made some listeners cringe with embarrassment. Admittedly, the public would later demonstrate their appetite for novelty acts – correct tune optional – such as Jedward by making the unlikely pair millionaires. However, few would admit to being one of the 3.5 million people that had bought a copy of the twins' album – a figure equivalent to almost a fifteenth of the British population. In spite of the popularity of such acts, Jessie wanted to be recognised as a credible artist – and with that in mind, perhaps she'd been on the wrong label to begin with.

Nevertheless, that didn't make the news any less distressing. "Someone told me on the telephone – they've gone into liquidation. I didn't even know what that meant!" Jessie exclaimed of the moment. "Liquidisation? What, they've been turned into a soup?"

Jessie was devastated. Yet within days of hearing the news, she was out on the road again, this time supporting Girls Aloud on their Tangled Up tour. Still reeling from the shock of losing her record contract, she threw herself into the shows wholeheartedly. Yet there was a question mark over whether Jessie would appeal to Girls Aloud's audiences.

The girls were turning up the temperature with their usual brand of prick-tease pop, featuring salacious costumes and scantily clad dance routines. Their efforts would see *The Mirror* describe the tour as "their most sexually charged performances yet". However, while Girls Aloud projected a persona that was sexy yet submissive, Jessie was going for a vibe that was sassy, strong and self-confident. While they were obligingly shaking their booty in candy-coloured pastel mini dresses, Jessie's all-black numbers were more power-dressing than provocative.

Even in a leotard, sheer black tights and ludicrously high killer heels, there seemed to be something macho about Jessie – she was a fighter making a statement. And perhaps that was true in every sense of the word – these were the last shows she'd perform courtesy of Gut and, if she didn't get re-signed, her stage career might be over there and then. But Jessie wouldn't be going out without a fight – and on those nights, she'd be stepping out to reclaim her career.

While Jessie was thrilled to be in the spotlight, she was plagued by nerves and unsure whether she and Girls Aloud were a good match. In the early days, she had been known for "raw" and "organic" performances without gimmicks. Girls Aloud, on the other hand, were embarking on their biggest tour yet, with a bank balance-busting £3 million budget and a £250,000 spend on pyrotechnics alone. Meanwhile, Jessie didn't have a single prop.

Then there was the material. All of her songs were self-written or co-written and based on personal experiences – she wasn't reading from a script. Whether she was singing about pain or triumph, the emotions belonged not just to her producers but to her. While Girls Aloud were performing their tunes, Jessie seemed to actually be living hers. It made for an authentic warts-and-all experience, but was it what Girls Aloud fans – arguably out for a night of light-hearted fun – were looking for?

What was more, their songs and costumes might have irritated someone who shared Jessie's feminist values. They had typecast themselves in turn as sex objects ('Love Machine'), bimbos ('Can't Speak French') and hopeless romantics ('I'll Stand By You'). It was a hardcore feminist's nightmare – and Jessie wasn't too pleased either. She would later go on to argue that she was "fed up with the way women have to sell themselves to be noticed" and that successful artists should "feel confident" and shouldn't "just be girly". She was channelling a persona that reflected that, with even hard-hitting reggae creeping into her shows.

The Girls Aloud tour portrayed a larger-than-life fantasy – a fashion statement for the girls and a wet dream for the boys – but Jessie rejected the notion of being an air-brushed diva. With all the differences that stood between them, would Jessie be successful at winning over new fans from the shows? How would she fare in their world?

Would the crowd – a mixture of panting adolescent males and hysterical preteen girls clutching banners – really warm to Jessie? After all, they weren't her usual audience. For the most part she needn't have worried, receiving generous applause. Perhaps the most nerve-racking night of the tour, however, was playing Harewood House in Leeds on August 29, 2008. It was a huge country mansion that had been home both to injured victims of the First and Second World Wars and even to a princess, the daughter of King George V and Queen Mary. The venue might have once housed royalty, but – that night – Jessie was no princess.

Keen to see the main attraction, the crowds were lukewarm towards her. Met with a chorus of boos, she hit back. "Boo as loud as you want," she retorted, "but I'll boo back!"

She fared better when, less than a month later, she found herself in Japan, touring with Cyndi Lauper. A singer who actively supported gay and transgender rights and had once had her tours sponsored by equality charities, she'd found Jessie on YouTube and had instantly warmed to her. She partnered her for a few dates in Japan, followed by a stint in the UK and Europe.

"I remember turning up to soundcheck [at the first show]," Jessie recalled to VEVO. "She was on stage talking to her band and then she turned to me and went: 'Are you the girl?' I was like: 'Okay, I'll be the girl if that's what you want me to be!' and she was like: 'I saw you sing on YouTube, you're amazing!'"

Jessie might have just been dumped by her label, but someone she'd admired since childhood had just revealed that she was a fan of her work – it wasn't all bad. The highlight for Jessie was playing with Cyndi at London's Shepherds Bush Empire in October 2008 when she'd been invited to duet with her on the tune 'Girls Just Want To Have Fun'.

"She's one of those people that's legendary," Jessie praised. "'Girls Just Want To Have Fun' was an anthem for me and it was brought out before I was born, but I didn't wanna tell her that! She came into my dressing room after I'd performed and was like: 'Do you wanna sing 'Girls' with me?'"

It was a heart-pounding moment. As much as she loved singing along as a child, it had been years since she'd heard the track. However, an offer from Cyndi wasn't one she was ready to turn down. Jessie got straight onto YouTube for a last-minute cramming session. Unlike the old days, it wasn't just her friends and family who'd hear her – if she messed up, she'd have several thousand witnesses to answer to. "My first reaction was: 'I'd better learn it because I don't know it!'" Jessie joked. "You know when you know some of it but you don't know it properly? So I went on YouTube and I was like: 'What bits do you want me to sing?'"

She was invited to join in on the harmonies, but Jessie came in too early on the second verse, leaving Cyndi's band struggling to catch up with her. "I came in on the wrong verse," she blushed. "I was like: 'Okay, just roll with it' – gasp! [But] it's a pleasure when people like that accept and bring through young people who are really trying to come through. Her fans were a bit confused [though], like, 'Who's that girl?'"

However, despite her timing blunder and the challenges of performing to a crowd who barely knew who she was, Jessie had a formidable stage presence. As soon as she arrived on stage, the arena rang out with rapturous applause. "She became a serious contender for the crowd's attention," a concert-goer told the author. "At one point, she was getting an even bigger reaction than Cyndi. You should have heard the cheers when she first came on! I think the crowd was looking for young, fresh energy – new blood – and she was giving it!"

That year, she also took to the stage for Conner Reeves, a UK songwriter and Brit Award winner who'd supported Whitney Houston and penned tracks for Joss Stone. In honour of the situation, Jessie performed a Whitney cover herself, adding 'I Have Nothing' to her set each night.

It'd been a success, but underneath the elation of the live shows, Jessie was secretly worried sick. She'd been struggling to get signed again, ever since she'd parted ways with Gut and with the large number of female artists already dominating the chart scene, Jessie feared she'd simply disappear in the crowd. At just 20, she was already looking failure in the face.

"It's really hard because you see the amount of people in this world that do something that are never able to call it their job – like their career and their hobby combined," Jessie told Clayton Perry, "like dancers that spend day in and day out rehearsing and dancing and training and they'll never get lots of jobs – not because they're not good, but just because that's the way it goes, sometimes."

Was Jessie about to join the ranks of the failed performers she spoke of? Only time would tell. She'd won a Sony ATV Worldwide publishing contract on the strength of the songs she'd written for Gut, so her time with them hadn't been a wasted journey – but she still had no record deal. Tensions with her management were also spilling over to muddy the waters. "Sometimes you're not always surrounded with people pushing you and believing in you," Jessie continued. "My mum and dad always did, but they weren't the ones who were looking after my career."

By this time, Jessie was considering abandoning the music industry altogether. With Gut, she'd played 300 gigs and seven support tours and had showcased her work with the most prestigious top-selling artists – yet she was still penniless. She'd composed more than 150 songs in just two years but lacked confidence in herself as a writer – and the unkind comments were coming thick and fast.

Yet Jessie was her own worst critic – according to her, some of her efforts were "so shockingly bad that I'd delete them off iTunes before anyone had the chance to see them". The two biggest dips in her confidence had been lying helplessly in a hospital bed with a stroke, cancelling gigs until she could recover and then losing her contract with Gut just two weeks before the single was due to be released.

Yet, according to a former employee for the defunct label, Jessie should have been thankful that she didn't start her career as a Gut artist. "Thank God that didn't happen!" she revealed to the author. "Jessie was agonising over what could have been, if only she'd been released a few months earlier before it all happened – at least that way she'd have a CD out – but she didn't realise how lucky she was. Gut's budget was close to non-existent even back in the days when they signed her. The company was struggling with huge debts and didn't have the money to promote her or give her the proper attention-grabbing launch that she deserved. If the CD had gone earlier, she'd have flopped instantly because of the lack of money. However, I think it showed what a standout singer Jessie really was that she was signed up without hesitation even when money was so scarce."

She added: "Jessie didn't realise that at the time and, in her enthusiasm to see her star rising, she didn't really understand the business side of things. In her eyes, it was all about getting her work out there as soon as possible, regardless of the climate, while we were trying to formulate the best possible conditions for her to be a success."

If Jessie had been eager back then, it wasn't the same at all a few months later. Feeling she was destined to be a support act forever instead of making it on her own, she began to reassess what she was doing.

"There were a lot of tears," Jessie revealed to *I Like Music*, "and a lot of moments thinking: 'I can't do this, I've got no money, I don't see my family and friends, I don't sleep, what am I doing this for?' The only reason I ever carried on was for my mum and my dad and my family – and also my fans – if it was one of them or 15,000 of them. I just thought if I could inspire one young girl or young boy, then that's why I was doing what I was doing."

However, the memory of why she wanted to be a star – to inspire and support others – was fading, one sleepless night after another. With Sony, it was the same combination of writing and gigging and benign optimism, but it seemed to be a road to nowhere. In fact, she'd even taken to camping out in a car to try to make it. "I [was] doing support stuff in any place I could around the world for free," Jessie told *The Mirror* of her early hustle. "All the while, I was just living in a car. Doing all that stuff felt so crazy… yet these are the things you have to go through to be the kind of artist you want to be, the type of artist who survives in this industry."

Still unsure of whether she was strong enough to be an artist, Jessie wondered if she should return to her comfort zone in musical theatre, or perhaps even work behind the scenes. She wasn't sure she was cut out for such a tough industry. However, knowing that she had even just a handful of listeners friending her on Facebook kept her motivated.

"I never, ever gave up because of my fans," Jessie told Clayton Perry. "Even when I had 10! I just feel like you owe it to your fans, however many you have. Every artist in the world that exists has at least a hundred fans, and every single one of those people's lives you can change. And there have been so many times I have wanted to give up, because people don't see behind the scenes – the hard days and the no sleep and constantly having to give things up… but you have to look at it in a bigger picture and go: 'You know what? I owe this to so many more people and I've been brought up better than to give up.'"

Gathering all the strength she had, Jessie put herself out there again – only to be bitterly disappointed by the reaction from record labels. The year 2008 was owned by women. At one point, nine of the top 10 singers in the chart were female. Amy Winehouse was still riding high on the success of *Back To Black*, released two years previously, and – back then – her label had hope for another album before the year was out. Early live versions of Jessie's song 'Stand Up' bore a similarity to Amy's 'Just Friends' but – as she went on to claim a record-breaking five Grammy Awards in one night – there was no room for another Amy.

Meanwhile Adele's soul tunes were also blaring out of every self-respecting radio station's playlist – and the British music industry was so consumed by the success of the soul divas they already had, that they didn't feel they needed another.

"Adele, Duffy and Amy were all out at that time," Jessie despaired to *Flavour* magazine. "No one wanted to sign another UK female artist." Jessie went to every label there was – from small and independent companies to major household names backed by billion-dollar budgets – but, one by one, all of them turned her down. "They weren't interested," she recalled to *The Daily Record*. "They said they didn't get it and didn't think they could work with me. A lot of girls were about to dominate the industry at the time and I felt I had missed my chance."

She needn't have worried. The UK might have declined but people were watching her with interest from much further afield. Sony producer Rich Christina, convinced that Jessie could make it, had sent a link to Jessie's Myspace page to industry superstar Jason Flom. Trying to attract the attention of Jason was aiming high – but his interest would be a green light to any artist that they had the wow factor. Jason had discovered The Corrs, Katy Perry and Kid Rock, all of whom had gone on to enjoy glittering careers. He'd also developed KT Tunstall and Paramore – in fact, almost everyone he'd worked with seemed to have made it big.

At the time of receiving the link to Jessie's page, Jason had just founded a new company in the USA, Lava Records – and he was looking for new signings. He and his right-hand man Harinder Rana "listened to it and loved it". At the time, Harinder had been a junior colleague desperate to impress. In his eagerness to win a job with Jason, he'd sent him a set of golf balls and a golf glove with his name embroidered on it. To some it was an unbearable display of ass-kissing, but it worked – and he was offered a job.

Once there, Harinder was motivated to rise in the ranks and make a name for himself by discovering the next big talent – and Jessie caught his eye. While most music industry employees were taking a well-earned break over the Christmas of 2008, Harinder was taking a 10-hour flight from LA to London to meet Jessie – and he hadn't told anyone in the office.

"Without even telling me, Harinder flew over to England on his own money and tracked down Jessie," Jason Flom recalled incredulously. "He then called me from a coffee shop in London and put her on the phone.

After speaking to me for the first time, she was like: 'This is different than everything I'd thought!' and was excited about the idea of working with us."

There was one barrier to that – Jessie's management at the time, who had been working to mastermind her career from a tiny basement in Brixton, South London, was forbidding her from having direct contact with labels. "They were insisting on a crazy deal," Jason groaned. "The situation was complicated because the management was not letting her speak directly to any labels."

However, Harinder had made the connection by seeking out Jessie himself. What was more, his interest urged Jessie to feel more confident about the string of rejections she'd received from labels in the UK. She now knew it was bad timing rather than a lack of talent that was losing her lucrative contracts – and it made all the difference. "When someone slams a door in my face, I try to find a bigger key or a chisel to try to break it down," she recalled to the *Daily Record*. "I knew that wasn't the end of me – it was the beginning."

Indeed, she found herself the flavour of the month in America – and began to realise that, while it wasn't what she'd had in mind, her showbiz career could have its humble beginnings there instead.

Before she could take that opportunity any further, she first had to take up an invitation from R&B performer Chris Brown. He was touring Europe for two weeks in January 2009 and was looking for a feisty support act. Jessie didn't need to be asked twice. "I think Chris is one of the most underrated artists. He's incredible," Jessie told Neon Limelight. "As a performer, he's disgustingly sick."

Much of the music-buying public agreed. He'd been in the game since 2005 and had already earned a reputation as a multimillion-selling artist with dance moves like Michael Jackson's. His songs were even out-performing those of his showbiz lover, Rihanna.

Just a couple of months later, the squeaky-clean persona he'd worked for years to build would come crashing down. He'd make headline news worldwide for assaulting Rihanna at a pre-Grammy Awards party, leaving her too bruised and battered to show up for the ceremony – and the music industry would be in shock.

It was only a matter of time before the cracks would begin to show in his seemingly perfect high-profile romance – but back in January, Chris could have done no wrong in the eyes of the public. He was due to play across the Netherlands to arenas of 10,000 fans per night and Jessie was about to join him.

"He booked me from YouTube!" she recalled to *I Like Music*. "That was probably the biggest and scariest [tour I ever did]. When I look back now, I think, 'Woah!' I can't believe I actually did that. I went there, just me and my mate [guitarist Ben Martinez] with an iTunes-burned CD wearing really high shoes and then I performed in front of 10,000 people. If I had to do that now, I'd be like: 'What am I gonna wear, I need make-up like this…' I just love the fact that was so organic. I don't think a lot of people get the opportunity to do something like that when they're not in the limelight, no one knows who they are, they're not being watched by the whole world. It was kind of a development deal in disguise."

Not being in the spotlight definitely had its advantages. If she fell flat on her face in her six-inch heels, there wouldn't be a gleeful press pack waiting to photograph the episode in all its embarrassing glory. They were more likely to cry: 'Jessie who?' before moving on to find a more lucrative singer. It wouldn't even be of interest to a low-key gossip forum. Accidentally flashing her underwear at an inopportune moment might have paid photographers' wages for a week if she'd been a celebrity – but, as an unknown support act, the shots would be almost totally worthless. If she came in on the wrong verse, as she had done during her duet with Cyndi Lauper, she wouldn't have to read about her mistakes the next day – it wouldn't even get a sentence on the reviews page.

No matter what she did, her misdemeanours went largely unnoticed. As an anonymous artist, this was the perfect way for her to learn the ropes without fear of ridicule.

It wasn't all good though – at times, she'd have to endure disdainful indifference or – even worse – downright hostility. Chris Brown's audiences in particular proved to be a mismatch for Jessie – and it was a trying tour. At first glance, the two acts might not have sounded wildly different from each other, but – on the night – disaster struck.

It was like the time Katy Perry braved the Warped Tour, a punk-rock festival for sweaty, abundantly tattooed macho men – while dressed as Lolita. It was akin to Slipknot putting in an appearance at the local nursing home, performing to pensioners expecting the soothing tones of Mantovani. It was more awkward than sending teetotal Jessie to an Alcoholics Anonymous meeting – they just wouldn't have anything to talk about.

Chris walked the fine line between edgy gangsta and pin-up poster boy. He had enough heartfelt ballads to make him parent friendly and he'd even hosted children's TV shows but, in spite of that, he was enormously popular with fans of an urban street sound. Teenage girls admired his rippling muscles when he tore off his shirt during live shows while his songs about stealing cars and speeding appealed to a more macho crowd, earning him hip-hop street cred. His audiences were divided between the hormonal girls who saw him as a lust object and the would-be tough guys who wanted to emulate him – and neither crowd was interested in Jessie.

The boos began – but she repeated the same technique she'd learned on the Girls Aloud tour, telling outraged punters she'd give as good as she got. "I remember getting booed because everyone wanted to see the main act, so I just booed back," she laughed to *Closer*. "I said: 'I'm only here for 10 minutes, so if you like it, scream. If you don't, boo me, but I'll boo back as loud as you.'"

She swiftly turned her fate around as Chris's fans – perhaps admiring her nerve and audacious swagger – began to laugh. "You've got to believe in yourself and be confident," she added. "That was a great development for me to learn my craft without being in the limelight."

After that night, Jessie had five more shows to do with Chris and she was dreading more hostility. To her horror, she developed OCD as a reaction to the stress, running her tongue around her mouth 100 times on each side before taking to the stage. However, bizarre rituals aside, Jessie used her stage fright to her advantage. Like 50 Cent, who'd thanked his enemies for their hatred, saying it gave him energy and fuelled his work – Jessie found that negativity spurred her on. "I always turn nerves into adrenalin," she told Neon Limelight. "It was a case of: 'I own this right now and you're going to listen to me.'"

While she was centre stage, the audience could hardly have ignored her – and she felt a power rush. "I think that made me an amazing performer in the sense that it was that kind of pressure and being able to own the stage with just me and in front of 10,000 people a night and without a band and dancers and stuff, that's only going to make it better," Jessie added. "I'm glad I had to struggle in the beginning."

An anonymous friend agreed that the adversity had only made her stronger. "She loved showing how strong she was – a lesser artist would have cried or panicked or given up and gone home – but she didn't care," she revealed. "She was going to own the place, whether they liked it or not. Even if every person in that room hated her, her strength was one thing they could never take away from her. She knew standing up to those people would only make her a better artist in the future."

There was more angst in store in Amsterdam – in the drug-friendly Dutch capital, she would learn the occupational hazard of her job with a mistake the tabloids dubbed her "hash cake hospital hell".

Jessie's years of abstinence from drug culture had left her uninformed – and, when she entered a bar and saw a tempting cookie, she thought it was just that – a harmless snack. How wrong she was – and within minutes an ambulance was rushing her to hospital.

It was every parent's worst nightmare – their youngest daughter phoning from a hospital many miles from home following a drug overdose – but Jessie's mother took the news surprisingly well. "I had to call an ambulance because I was convulsing," she told *Closer*. "I called my mum and she was like: 'I'm glad you did it, because you'll never do it again.'"

What was more, Jessie's anguish at being booed was quickly subsiding altogether. "To some people I have the best voice in the world, to others I sound like a dying dolphin," she joked to Global Grind. "It's just taste. That's the best thing about the music industry – that everyone has their own likes and dislikes."

She'd also quickly learned that no one could have universal appeal. Being liked by everyone was impossible and wasn't even necessarily desirable. "Whatever you do, whoever you are, whatever race you are, whatever culture you are, whatever you like to do behind closed doors, what food you eat, how you live your life, someone is always going to have a problem with something," Jessie told Clayton Perry. "I've got my feet firmly on the ground with the fact that I know that people are going to hate me, and if they didn't, I'd be doing something wrong, because it's not humanly possible to have everybody love you and worship you, because that's weird. I think it's just having inner peace and being able to say: 'You know what? I'm not perfect, but nobody is, and I'm just going to do what I can and try my best.'"

After the Chris Brown tour, Jessie returned to the UK, but the British music industry "didn't really have the space for little old me". Desperately trying to fight for a place among the likes of Leona Lewis, Adele and Duffy and not really knowing where she fitted in, Jessie knew she needed a change.

"I think because the UK is so small, you can't really blend in," she told Global Grind. "You really have to stand out. Like, there can't be six of me if that makes sense… in the US you can afford to have artists that are very similar that don't need to be very original and I think in the UK people can sniff out someone who looks close to someone else."

While she knew she was different from other female artists out there, at that time, Jessie wasn't sure how to express it – and, as a result, the industry still hadn't sat up and taken notice. Yet Jessie's mantra was: "Everything happens for a reason."

"It was like my life was over, but my mum told me: 'When one door slams in your face, it means there's another one round the corner waiting to be opened… a golden ticket in disguise," Jessie told *Flavour*.

While listening to that advice, she remembered the positive experience she had had being headhunted by American labels a few months before. Without a backward glance, Jessie packed her bags and fled to the USA under the wing of the William Morris Talent Agency, which had offices in New York and LA. So what if the door that marked the entrance to her career wasn't exactly round the corner but happened to be several thousand miles away?

She stepped off the plane in New York resolving to "forget about all the crazy stuff that was going on". However, it wasn't just the near impossibility of getting signed to a label at home that was driving Jessie away – there was another reason that she'd kept undercover. "I kind of got the hump," she later admitted to BBC *Newsbeat*. "I was in America and I just disappeared. I didn't want people to think I'd run away from the UK." But why?

It hadn't just been a writing trip – according to those in the know, Jessie had run away with her lover. She'd known fellow singer Kira since age 17 and had been introduced to her during studio sessions with her producer Shae. The two had become inseparable and friendship had blossomed into sexual attraction, closely followed by love.

However, while Jessie's parents were comfortable with her sexuality – and most of her friends had come to terms with it too – not everyone felt the same. According to one friend, she found herself under pressure to be someone she wasn't to fit in with the demands of the industry. "Jessie might have been with boys in the past, but she is 100 per cent gay," she revealed to the author. "She was advised not to come out though. Certain people looking after her career thought that while being bi was trendy, exotic and a fashion statement, coming out as gay would alienate people, especially male fans. They wanted guys to buy into an illusion that if they met her one night after a show, they'd have a chance of being invited back for a two-girl threesome. That would increase her allure, whereas they thought being seen as gay could damage her popularity."

She added: "From the very beginning, Jessie was openly lesbian and didn't hide it from anyone, but as her career developed, she had some of the wrong people around her. They knew how important image was and they wanted to paint a fantasy on to her. They asked her to tone it down a bit, make some changes and just say that she wasn't labelling herself. That way if she was seen as a woman, it could be seen as just a bit of fun. There are so many homophobes out there that they feared a potentially career-damaging backlash, whereas being bisexual would instantly be seen as less threatening. Jessie was frightened of losing her connections and opportunities for fame, so she went along with it, but she was incensed that she was being asked to compromise herself like that. It also wasn't fair on her girlfriend at a time when they were getting serious about each other."

Ironically, Jessie's struggles had come at a time when swinging both ways was in fashion. However, while some in the industry were trying to persuade their protégée to like girls, some of Jessie's team were allegedly doing the opposite and doing everything in their power to keep her away from that image. Katy Perry's hit single 'I Kissed A Girl' had made the number one spot around the world, but the storyline portrayed her as just another heterosexual girl experimenting. However seductive her female crush might have been, she made it clear where her loyalties lay when she sang that she hoped her boyfriend didn't mind it. Katy was later photographed French kissing and dirty dancing with another girl – but seemingly only for the entertainment of her wide-eyed husband to be, Russell Brand, who was watching close by. That summed up what many believed to be the extent of Katy's sapphic fantasies – a motivation to get the attention of her man. While Katy's sexuality was portrayed as a non-threatening – and some might say manufactured – expression of male fantasies, Jessie's was the real deal.

She hadn't been trying to tease and titillate and it wasn't a stunt to turn heads. This was who she was, and she was sick and tired of hiding it. "A lot of people were against Jessie's relationship with Kira and they disapproved of it being out in the open," her friend continued. "Because this was a real relationship and not 'I kiss girls to turn my boyfriend on'. They thought it would intimidate fans but ironically for years it was Jessie who was intimidated, because she felt she had to hide who she was in order to get famous – but after years of trying, she still hadn't had her chance."

Jessie had fled to America not just to write songs and see if her luck was in stateside but to escape from the restraints that bound her back home. "You live once," Jessie had later commented to *PrideSource*, "and if you spend your whole life apologising for things that make you happy and always feeling like you have to explain yourself or justify what you love, then life's no fun."

Indeed, back in England, life hadn't been much fun. While her partner was putting her under pressure to be true to herself and come out to the world, some of the people handling Jessie's career were giving her a stark warning to the contrary. "You wouldn't think that in this day and age a woman would feel obliged to choose between her relationship and her career," her anonymous friend added, "but this was the reality for Jessie. Her and Kira used to sing the Destiny's Child song 'Survivor' together because singing was part of what their bond was, but also as a symbol that they could survive any obstacle that their relationship threw at them and still come out the other side."

Determined to make her relationship work, Jessie had hoped that America would be a fresh start for them both. She was taking a six-week working trip – three weeks in LA and three in New York – and Kira would be by her side. She hadn't expected to do any more than write, but when she arrived on US soil, things started moving fast.

"My manager at the time was like: 'We should do some gigs, let's do a showcase here and there,'" Jessie recalled to *I Like Music*. "I just thought: 'I hope the UK don't think I've run away.' It was the most amazing thing, but I didn't want people to think I'd ditched Britain and gone: 'I'm going to America, up yours!' I was taking British music to America to say: 'What do you think?'"

Jessie had always been an ambassador for the UK. A keen Spice Girls fan as a child, she'd taken to wearing clothes and accessories with the Union Jack symbol on it, like Geri Halliwell had done in the group, to prove her loyalty to her country.

In spite of that, the idea of US success was compelling. Making it big in the UK would be success on a minuscule scale back in America, a country where the state of Texas alone was bigger than Britain in its entirety. It was a fearsome challenge, but a very attractive one. While US artists such as Katy Perry and Lady Gaga were topping the charts in England, the charts in the USA were mainly dominated by home-grown talent – and she hoped to redress the balance. Even London R&B artist Estelle's attempts at flattery in the song 'American Boy', where she gushes of her lust for stateside men who can woo her with trips to Brooklyn and LA, didn't earn her much love across the pond.

Talking of the insular music industry, Jessie had told Clayton Perry: "I'm honoured to be British [but] I just feel like pop icon wise, there's no one in the UK that's really sitting with Rihanna and Beyoncé and Katy and P!nk and really kind of just flying."

Perhaps Jessie could be the one to change that – and she was certainly ready to try. "The reason I'm bringing [my music] to the US is because why shouldn't I?" she added defiantly. "I want to take the British flag and fly it around the globe – and America had better be ready for me, because I'm coming!"

Chapter 6

Taking Hollywood On
Her Own Terms

*"When I'm in the studio sometimes, I think, no, I don't need a therapist –
I just need to write a great song!"*

Jessie J

The first step to conquering America and inducing record labels to sit up and take notice was to play the showcases her manager had suggested. Jessie was up to the challenge and three shows were hastily arranged in LA, New York and San Francisco. The first of these was scheduled for April 28, 2009 at LA's legendary Viper Room – and it was a good place to start.

Located on Hollywood's Sunset Strip, it was one of the most notorious nightclubs in LA's history, boasting decadence and debauchery with a rock'n'roll soundtrack. Anyone who was anyone on the Hollywood music scene had been there before.

Of course, there were some similarities with Jessie's home town. The club had been home to more catfights than the average Essex bar, but instead of playing host to the occasional glamour model, socialite or Z-list actor, the Viper Room was packed full to the rafters with high-profile names on any given night – this was Hollywood in the raw. There were more celebrities and bigger egos.

The club saw its fair share of drama too, which could only be expected for a city best known for its movie scene. Some of the city's gargantuan egos came into play within a year of the club's opening in 1993 when a photographer was reportedly savaged by Mötley Crüe singer Tommy Lee for snapping him with his then wife, Pamela Anderson.

History repeated itself when another photographer snapped an incriminating picture of an embrace between Rolling Stones singer Mick Jagger and Pulp Fiction actress Uma Thurman – one so steamy that the paparazzi claimed it was worth $1 million – and Mick's bodyguard wrestled him to the ground, ordering the club to confiscate his film. Big egos translated to big bucks and an expensive lawsuit followed, seeing the club pay out $600,000.

The drama continued when *Baywatch* star Nicole Eggert got physical with a mystery woman over a mutual boyfriend. All the drunken violence seemed to simply add to the club's notoriety – after all, people reasoned, what was a little drama between celebrities? It made for good gossip column headlines, at any rate.

Yet the hotspot was also home to tragedy. In 1993, the same year it opened, troubled actor River Phoenix passed away from a drugs overdose, collapsing in the street outside in the early hours of Halloween morning.

The club was part owned by fellow actor Johnny Depp, whose whirlwind romance with model Kate Moss saw the pair boast that they'd christened every room of the nearby Chateau Marmont hotel with their lovemaking, one ludicrously expensive and equally decadent suite at a time. This part of LA was renowned for hedonism, celebrity style.

Yet while the hotel might have been good for orgasms, the Viper Room was just as good for eargasms. Oasis, Courtney Love, Iggy Pop, John Mayer, The Pussycat Dolls and The Red Hot Chili Peppers had all played at the club before, a record that led the *Los Angeles Times* to admiringly describe the nightspot as "the most consistently hip club in town".

Meanwhile, even the audience had previously included stars as bright and prestigious as Gwen Stefani, Christina Aguilera and Cameron Diaz. Yet on the night of Jessie's showcase, A-list actresses and the top drawer of musical celebrities were the least of her worries. Instead, the room was filled with record-label bosses, music critics and other key players in the industry – the ones who had the power to make or break her career – and the thought of it had her heart pounding.

Mainstream success might have seemed elusive and far away in a country the size of America, but the people watching her that night really did have the resources and say-so to pluck her from anonymity and turn her into a star. Jason Flom, the founder and CEO of Lava Records, was in the audience, and he'd picked up Katy Perry on the basis of a showcase here. Less than two months later, she'd made her mark as an international artist. The right performance here could open doors for Jessie too.

She might have been teetotal and she couldn't promise the paps their wet dreams of a drunken collapse or an uninhibited catfight, claws drawn, outside the club's front door, but she was on a mission to prove her music was just as tantalising as those whose lifestyles were emblazoned across the headlines. She took to the stage without gimmicks, props or a history of rock'n'roll naughtiness – and commanded the attention of the crowd nonetheless.

She began the show with 'Big White Room', which she described elusively as "a song about a personal situation", and went on to perform the velvety voiced jazzy number 'Sexy Silk', about a liaison with a hot date. A song that Gut had earmarked as a potential single, it had the vintage-style sound of a topless revue, the musical-style extravagance of a standard like 'Big Spender' and the feel of old-school tracks such as 'Fever', as performed by Peggy Lee or 'I Just Wanna Make Love To You', as performed by Etta James. Viewers might almost have expected to see a Dita Von Teese lookalike shimmying across the stage in little more than red lipstick and suspenders.

Track by track, Jessie was introducing the audience to her world, and the set she'd chosen meant there were some surprises in store for those expecting a list of generic pop tracks.

"One thing we could see straight away was the diversity of the songs," an anonymous member of the crowd told the author admiringly. "We were enthralled. Most artists have a trademark sound and in the worst case scenario, we see them go through song after song in the same style and the same key. Some hopefuls make us wanna yawn five minutes into their set, because we can't tell the difference between one song and another. Jessie could turn her hand to anything from an R&B/soul song to a weepy ballad to a bit of ethnic music. That told us there was nothing we could throw at her that she wouldn't be able to cope with."

She added: "While there's obviously nothing wrong with having a trademark sound to set yourself apart from the rest, it's also a big plus if you can show your skills go beyond one type of music."

Jessie was attracting just as much admiration at a secret venue in nearby San Francisco and then at SOB's restaurant and nightclub in New York. The latter saw her meet R&B singer and Rihanna lookalike Cherri V, an aspiring pop star with flaming red hair and, on occasion, red-tinted eyebrows too. The two, both from the UK, sparked up a firm friendship. It wasn't just fellow singers she was networking with, but a plethora of industry names.

Her show in LA had a glowing review from A&R Worldwide, which claimed: "One hates to invoke the ghost of Janis Joplin, but Jessie J has that blues-based shouting style down cold, while still managing to hit notes that the Southern Comfort-loving Janis could only dream about nailing herself."

What was more, as an anti-drugs campaigner, Jessie didn't have the same appetite for self-destruction as her late rival either. Janis had joined the 27 Club after a long battle with heartbreak and substance abuse, dying before her twenty-eighth birthday. But Jessie was hoping to be around a lot longer – and this was just the beginning.

She'd transformed from the girl that nobody in the business had wanted to give the time of day to, into one that had eight offers of a record deal on the table within a matter of days. "Within two days of the showcases in New York and LA, I found myself sitting with the head of every label in the US," she told the *Daily Record*. "They were calling back to the UK saying: 'Excuse me, did you meet Jessie J and not bother signing her?' I felt like a snitch! There I was, sitting with Clive Davis, who signed Whitney Houston."

However, the adrenalin couldn't go to her head too much, as it was time to decide on who to sign with. While she'd attracted a lot of attention, one label boss who'd entered the bidding war was particularly keen: Jason Flom. "It was very competitive," he recalled. "[I offered her] a very strong deal, especially in today's climate, but I felt like I might never find another artist as gifted as Jessie J."

By this time, Jessie had parted ways with her original mentors, 141a Management, and had been liberated from the arrangement said to forbid her from direct contact with labels, so she was sitting around the table, soaking up the compliments for herself.

She was torn, as she could barely refuse the opportunity of a lifetime to become a recording artist on American soil, but she also felt guilty for not representing the UK. After some soul-searching, she made her decision, supported by her new management team at Crown Music. "Basically, I thought that this kind of opportunity doesn't come along very often in the industry so I decided to sign to the US label [the Jason Flom-fronted Lava Records] but on a worldwide deal, so I had a UK label as well," Jessie told *Gigwise*.

The deal saw her represented by Island Republic in England, the same label that had scooped up Amy Winehouse. She was clearly among musical royalty. "Darcus Beese and Ted Cockle at Island were so excited about Jessie from the beginning," Jason marvelled.

No sooner had she flown home to share the good news with family and friends, than it was time to return to the US and show she meant business with a three-month writing trip for her debut album. What was more, it wasn't a moment too soon – American websites were already praising her "commercially friendly yet edgy alt-pop sound, [which] has been described by some music taste-makers as a Lily Allen with mainstream accessibility" - and she wanted to justify the hype.

What she hadn't bargained on was the crippling loneliness. Jetting around an unknown country to fulfil the dreams of a lifetime wasn't what it was cracked up to be. While her beloved Kira was present for part of her trip, flying out for her birthday and accompanying her to the annual lesbian and gay empowerment event LA Pride, on June 13, 2009, for much of her stay she was alone.

Her saving grace was YouTube. To combat her homesickness, she began engaging with people online, singing to the screen whenever she felt sad and uploading her videos to get an instant reaction.

"I got addicted to putting up videos on YouTube, because it gives you that quick, instant 'what do people think?'" Jessie told *I Like Music*. "That was the best thing because people were like: 'I'm not sure about this, we prefer this and we prefer that.' I think YouTube taught me that people loved not only me singing but me talking. I think people point and laugh more than join in though! But yeah, I enjoyed that connection, like a friendship – this personal thing that me and my fans had that no one else had really discovered."

She'd been living alone in an apartment in downtown LA that her management had found for her and, despite getting the VIP treatment when she was in the studio, she wasn't immune from feeling isolated and alone. That was when, against the advice of her label, she posted her first song, 'Big White Room', on her YouTube account. "My label were like: 'Don't do it, wait!' and I was like: 'No! I wanna skip you out, skip management out, skip PR out, skip anyone else out and go straight to the people, straight to my fans, straight to an honest opinion!'" she added.

To some, this was career suicide. In an age when illegal downloads and song leakages were wrecking people's career prospects and downsizing their potential royalties, Jessie seemed to have no fear about sharing her songs for free, all before the big moment for her album's release had arrived. But she had no regrets.

"I'm glad I did it," she continued. "Some people hated it and I loved that, and some people hated it and I loved that [too]. I never wanted to be in between with people going: 'Hmm, not sure.' Either hate me or love me, they're two passionate feelings, that's what I want."

She defended her decision further when she told Neon Limelight: "I just think I kind of opened the gate before the label did... I just always wanted to do this organically. I didn't want to be one of these artists with this massive launch and they just kind of came out of nowhere and everyone goes, like: 'Who is that chick?' I kind of like the fact that people can go on YouTube and see [my videos from the beginning]."

According to one anonymous industry insider, the decision to release her early efforts – even the ones as unglamorous as the unplugged singing sessions in her tiny LA bathroom – hadn't damaged her prospects one bit. In fact, she felt it had merely added to the buzz-building process.

"People loved that Jessie was interactive," she revealed. "People are gonna download songs for free anyway – they don't care about artists' profits – whereas Jessie was more open about giving away her songs. Instead of resenting her and seeing her as a faraway star, they appreciated that she was sharing her journey from the beginning. They saw her as just like them – someone who was human, someone who got nervous like they did, and who was just an ordinary girl, albeit one with an extraordinary talent."

She added: "Some people make the mistake of wanting to give off an image of perfection at all times. Fans don't always want perfection – they want something they can relate to. The thing that Jessie did right was to treat herself like she was one of them and show herself in the raw, feeling blue, singing in her apartment to shake off the blues, like they probably did themselves – even the non-singers. She was relatable, rather than some anonymous, pretentious, snobbish personality hidden behind her label. People really warmed to her for that. I'm sure the more cautious people safe-guarding her career would have warned her off, but in this case I think releasing tracks early was the best thing she could ever have done."

For Jessie, meanwhile, releasing her material wasn't just a business decision to build up her fanbase and bond with them. It was a form of therapy. Despite her excitement, she was feeling insecure in LA. To add to her misery, she was also struggling to make friends in the city. There was a fiercely competitive atmosphere and she was eyed with suspicion and even jealousy when the other girls heard her distinctive English accent. She was instantly pigeonholed as a transatlantic jet-setter who might be on the brink of making it in a place where making it was rare. Therefore, to some, she was the enemy.

"LA is an amazing place, but it's very cliquey, people have their friends and as soon as they heard my voice, they knew I was there for something," she confided to *I Like Music*. "I ended up [puts on American accent] 'talking like this' by the end of the trip because then people wouldn't ask me so many questions. So I kind of learned to have this decent American accent. I don't think it's that bad!"

No such pretence was needed in the studio – when she met Polish-American super producer Dr. Luke, she bonded with him instantly.

"I remember being told, like, you know, 'Luke is kind of very intense, just take it slow' but I kind of went in and was like: 'What's up? Like, hello!'" Jessie joked to 3 News.

A collaboration with Dr. Luke seemed to go hand in hand with a golden ticket to stardom, an access-all-areas pass to the top of the charts. The multimillionaire had co-written songs like 'I Kissed A Girl' and 'Hot And Cold' for Katy Perry, 'Circus' for Britney Spears, 'Who Knew' and 'U And Ur Hand' for P!nk, 'About You Now' for the Sugababes and 'Since U Been Gone' for Kelly Clarkson.

One of his biggest claims to fame, however, was writing 'Tik Tok', the first single for American performer Ke$ha, which became the world's longest-running number-one debut single for a female performer since 1977. He'd more than proved his talent in the pop and R&B camp, but he'd also written for hip-hop giant Mos Def, counter-cultural Lady Sovereign and tender ballad kings The Backstreet Boys. *Billboard* magazine listed him as one of the top 10 producers of the decade. It seemed there was nothing he couldn't turn his hand to – and Jessie was keen to try a piece of the pie.

The marriage of Jessie's writing skills and Dr. Luke's hit-making instincts began with 'Party In The USA'. Also joining them in the studio was Claude Kelly, another well-known producer whose claims to fame included sessions with Katy Perry and Rihanna – and the atmosphere was electric.

"That was my first week of writing after I signed to Republic," Jessie told *Associated Press*. "It was the first big kind of writing session for my debut album and it was one of the first songs we did."

She'd wanted to write a song about her experiences coming to America for the first time to pursue her dreams and bottle that feeling on CD. "'Party In The USA' is about how excited I was to come to the US and how nervous I was and how I had butterflies all the time," she recalled to Global Grind. "I got in a cab outside of JFK [airport] and Jay-Z was on the radio, you know?"

It might have sounded like a mundane detail but her team thought it was a winning formula for a song. That said, Jessie was keen to avoid falling into the trap of entering a songwriter's bubble and living an existence that would see her bundled from studio to concert to hotel to airport and back again – she felt that would leave her bereft of authentic real life experiences to inspire her. "I have to make sure my life is exciting, because I don't want the next album to be about sitting in a hotel or on aeroplanes eating sushi and salad," she added. "You know, you have to live life to write about it."

Perhaps that was the reason that 'Party In The USA' didn't click with Jessie or her label for her. "I remember thinking this song was amazing, but I don't know if it's me 110 per cent," she recalled to 3 News. "It was cool, but it wasn't edgy enough."

The label felt the same – to them, it was an instant hit, but from Jessie they'd been expecting something a little more cutting-edge and unusual. "They said it was a great song and a hit, but they weren't sure if it was right for me," she recalled. "[But] Disney flew out as soon as they heard it."

The song was signed over to pop singer and ex-*Hannah Montana* actress Miley Cyrus and Jessie thought little more of it, focusing on finding a track that was "less pop" and a better fit.

Her mistake taught Jessie to be more assertive about what she did and didn't want, and she needn't have been afraid to make her tracks personal. A feel-good song about striding out of an airport on top of the world while Jay-Z's '99 Problems' blared out of the speakers of a bright yellow taxi was all very well, but Jessie needed to put more of herself into her songs. She wasn't just another party girl, nor was she going to play the part of an archetypal gangsta's moll in a hip-hop video, weeping that her man was locked up, or writhe provocatively on a beach in a bikini for the viewing pleasure of a male rapper.

"It's about learning what suits you and what doesn't," Jessie reflected to *Flavour*. "I could have been in bikinis singing 'Up In The Club' but that's not what I wanted to do. You've got to be true to who you are."

Lesson learned, Jessie didn't want to spend any more studio time on wasted efforts. She knew what she wanted and, no matter how nerve-racking it was, it was time to get tough.

"It's big pressure when you know you're going in with someone that's written huge hits for other female artists and you know you don't want to sound like them," she confessed to 3 News. "I went in with [Dr. Luke] and Claude, and said: 'This is who I am. This is what I do.'"

Dr. Luke responded positively, telling her he "appreciated her honesty" and the two began to scour her collection of iTunes downloads to find a sound she wanted to emulate in her own way. "We sat for hours and listened to like, old Mary J. Blige and old Mariah [Carey] and Whitney [Houston] and Lauryn [Hill] and I said: 'I kind of want to write tracks like that,'" she continued.

Within hours, the trio had composed 'Abracadabra', which Jessie proudly recalled was "very different to that big pop, Katy Perry, Britney Spears, Ke$ha kind of sound" – in fact, most of the major artists Dr. Luke had worked with. She'd successfully managed to subvert the sound of one of the most renowned producers in the game, days into her first recording session.

What was more, 'Abracadabra' had an unconventional subject matter too. "That was at a time when I was very happy in my life and comfortable in a relationship and that's when you know you're in love – when you wanna write songs about it," Jessie confided. But of course, this was no ordinary love song – it was a lesbian love song about Jessie's all-consuming infatuation with Kira.

She'd strived to create something "a bit throw-back... a bit showgirl" with traces of SUV, TLC and old-school Mariah Carey for a vintage all-American R&B sounds of the nineties vibe. However, perhaps she hadn't just wanted to distance herself from the ultra-modern Katy Perry and her club beats in sound, but in style too. 'Abracadabra' was no faux lesbian marketing ploy – inspired by her real life sapphic relationship, Jessie had meant every word from the heart.

'Nobody's Perfect' was another song where Jessie took control of the content. The track conjured up images of an apology for infidelity, but, according to Jessie, she'd had a very different subject matter in mind. "I've never tried to make anything up, like when I wrote 'Nobody's Perfect'. Claude said: 'We should make this into a relationship song' and I said: 'No, that's not what it's about!'" she explained.

So what was the tune about? Although Jessie was against bitchiness and back-stabbing, and rolled her eyes at the relentless rumour mill, she had realised that sometimes she was prone to a game of Chinese Whispers too, and with painful consequences. "It's about me chatting crap behind one of my good friend's backs and me telling too many people and it got back to them and the only person that was left hurting was me," she confessed to MSN.

Indeed, her unintentionally acidic tongue had got the better of her at the BRIT School too when she'd jokingly called a girl "fat" in the cafeteria at lunchtime, only to find that the victim of her words was standing right behind her. A blushing Jessie had been forced to change her words to "voluptuous" and make a shame-faced apology.

She'd also got herself into hot water when remarks she made about a fellow pupil bringing a bottle of vodka into the school for a party later that evening soon saw her branded as an alcoholic.

Her increasingly loose-lipped temperament could often get the better of her, but she'd always meant well. It was one round of verbal missiles in particular, however, that had inspired the song. "One thing it taught me is that everyone has someone they can trust," she explained of the private comments she'd made that had turned into a widespread rumour. "If you tell someone something about someone that you don't want them to know, that person will tell someone they trust, who'll tell someone they trust and it goes on and it spirals. I think it's good to vent but it's good to vent to people that have got your back. It was my fault and I needed to learn from it. That song was my apology."

She added: "It's important to sometimes talk about your flaws and the things that don't make you perfect. I'm not super-human. I'm not a superhero. I make mistakes."

Some might have been surprised at Jessie's confessional style in a music world where the emphasis was on perfection but, determined to use her music as therapy rather than to gloss over the truth to make a sparkling impression, she was on a quest for honesty. However, she realised she needed to avoid the temptation to create drama in her life simply to inspire new songs.

Whereas fellow British singer Lily Allen had once confessed to deliberately shaking up her relationships to bring on the heartbreak so that she would have a sad song in the making, Jessie feared she would get bored without the constant drama. "I try to make my life as interesting as possible without losing all my friends to be able to write a great album!" she guffawed.

Meanwhile, another theme had been taking shape in Jessie's mind for a song called 'Rainbow', which she would go on to record with a trio of producers: Warren Felder, Edwin Serrano and Kasia Livingston. She'd written an early version of it before she signed to her label and had been trying to improve it ever since. It had started out as a "love letter to the gay community", with Jessie revealing to *PrideSource*: "Whatever your sexuality, whatever your culture, whatever your race, everybody's the same. It's about – not everyone being gay, because that's not true, but everybody being from the same rainbow. We all have to share a pot of gold, we're all on the same yellow brick road."

Like Lauryn Hill, many of Jessie's songs had plots or told meaningful stories to draw attention to political or social issues. Yet 'Rainbow' was the one that was most symbolic of her desire to emulate Lauryn in making music that was "educational but not preachy".

In the song, Jessie described a wealthy man who might seem to be the object of everyone's envy, but countered that he too suffered and at times would feel "blue". She talked of his blood "bleeding red" like hers, perhaps in a nod to Shylock, a character in the Shakespeare play *The Merchant Of Venice*. He implores: "If you prick us, do we not bleed?" after experiencing prejudice for being Jewish – and, indeed, one of the central themes of 'Rainbow' was a fight back against prejudice.

Calling upon people to embrace their similarities instead of their differences, Jessie explained: "I was feeling like the world needs to pull together, wherever you are and whether you've got loads of money or you don't, whether you're on the dole or you're not, or you've got a part-time job, a full-time job, black, white, Chinese – whoever you are."

The song seemed to offer up music as the universal language, something that anyone could join in with regardless of who they were. Jessie seemed to be pointing out that everyone goes through love, pain, heartbreak, joy and sorrow and that emotions are universal to people from every walk of life. Whether the listener was, for example, an HIV-positive prostitute living on the poverty line in war-ravaged East Africa, or a multibillionaire whose biggest concern seemed to be no more pressing than what colour Ferrari to buy next for his collection, both shared humanity.

The song was very similar to the 2001 single 'What Would You Do?' by City High in its ability to tell hard-hitting stories about social dilemmas that provoked thought. That track recounts the fictional but true-to-life tale of a young woman forced to turn to prostitution to feed her son after his crack-addicted father flits in and out of prison and spends the family's cash on drugs. An old school friend who spots the woman selling her body for "a buck" in a sleazy strip joint takes her outside for a talk, hoping to turn her back to a righteous path. He fends off her protests of a tough life, saying that if his mother can fight her way out of adversity in a moral way, then so can she.

Ironically, few people questioned the possible hypocrisy of the man who was willing to buy into the prostitute's sorrow by going to the club in the first place and then to talk one of the girls out of her way of life despite his presence seeming to implicitly condone it. Either way, the song – unlike many others of its time – provoked thought on social problems and how they were dealt with.

While some artists painted their lives the brightest shade of glamorous with songs about fast cars, beautiful women and expensive houses, Jessie wanted to focus on real life. She wanted to portray realistic aspirations and images of attainable happiness instead of alluding to things her listeners could never afford or relate to.

However, the rap game was full of odes to shameless materialism, where singers bragged about their out-of-control lifestyles. For example, Tinie Tempah spoke of jetting around the world, partying with royalty and popping champagne like his credit card "had no limit", in stark contrast to his own poverty-stricken background. He spoke of singing for monarchs and name-checked a list of luxurious tour locations – some might say he'd forgotten his roots and been seduced by fame.

Yet Tinie was just one example – the rap genre was rife with songs about expensive lifestyles and social superiority. Songs regularly aspired to nights of passion with Playboy bunny girls on beds blanketed with bank notes, but Jessie argued that this wasn't real life. Since rap in particular was infamous for its portrayal of "glam", Jessie's decision to involve a rapper – B.o.B – on the song 'Price Tag' was all the more surprising.

What had informed her choice? "B.o.B is so cool and has the charisma of 1,000 charismatic people," Jessie gushed to Global Grind. "He is the funniest guy to hang out with. Everything he was rapping about, I felt like if I was a male rapper, I would rap about – and I loved how honest he was in his music. It was honest enough for anyone to listen."

In Jessie's eyes, he didn't subscribe to glorifying a superficial superstar lifestyle – that wasn't what he stood for. What was more, that was exactly the subject that she wanted to tackle on 'Price Tag'. "This was my second session [with Dr. Luke and Claude Kelly] after we'd written 'Party In The USA' and we were like: 'The pressure is on!' Like, you know when you kinda go: 'How do we top 'Party In The USA'?" Jessie recalled.

Luckily, she had an idea. "I remember saying I really wanna write a song about how the [music] industry just feels like its based on money and what you've got and what you haven't got and percentages and people wearing sunglasses indoors – I never really understood that," she added.

The message of the song was that good artistry was more important than the pay cheque. Moreover, dancing to the latest tune might be more rewarding if the listener wasn't consumed by the need to look perfect doing so.

"When we finished, Dr. Luke was like: 'This is gonna be massive!'" Jessie recalled, "and I suppose when you get someone like Dr. Luke saying that, you have to believe it! It was one of those songs that just stuck around!"

However, there was one thing missing, and that was a guest voice. "We sat down and we were like: 'Right, this song is a feature'," Jessie continued to Global Grind, "and B.o.B was definitely someone who was on everybody's mind at that point."

However, Jessie didn't even have so much as a single out yet – her only claim to fame was that, like many other artists, she was signed to a major record label. Would that be enough to persuade one of the world's most wanted rappers to take on her tune? She needn't have worried. "When you're making an album [but you don't have any material out yet], it's a lot harder to go: 'Please believe in my project!' [but] B.o.B was one of the first people that said: 'Cool, I'll do it!' and it's not often you get a big American person like B.o.B featuring on a UK track, so it was a big honour," Jessie beamed.

Perhaps, for him too, it hadn't been all about the "money, money, money". As soon as she got the green light, Jessie pulled out all the stops to make a personal appearance in the studio. "How can you collaborate with someone if you don't meet them?" she later asked, incredulously. "I did five plane journeys in four days and flew around the USA to Buffalo, New York, all these different places I'd never been to, to make sure I was there when he recorded it," she explained. "I really wanted to be part of it and be in the studio and make sure he felt like it was a proper creative experience and not: 'Yeah, my people holler at your people!'"

Once B.o.B had played his part and the pressure was off, the business relationship between Jessie and her two producers transformed into fun and games, with the two "cracking jokes" and "having scooter races in the car park". All three were self-confessed "big kids" at heart and the conversation had even led to talk about theme parks and Walt Disney World – the latter one of Jessie's dream holiday destinations.

However, the best moments came when the three began to relentlessly tease each other and put their taunts on tape. "We started taking the mickey out of Luke because all he does is eat coconuts," Jessie joked. "Literally, every five minutes he'll have loads of coconuts, like fresh ones, delivered to the studio – and I started calling him Coconut Tree."

His unorthodox appetite for the fruit, combined with Jessie's keen sense of humour, meant that teases and taunts were inevitable. "We were saying to him: 'When I wrote "I Kissed A Girl" I was under a coconut tree!'" she continued. "We just started making up this character. Then I called Claude Moonhead because he's got this massive head – literally, like a moon – and I've got like a pea head so they called me Pea. It was an in-joke. Like a secret joke, but now it's a very unsecret, out there joke!"

She was referring, of course, to the shout-out at the beginning of 'Price Tag' that name-checked the three's comedy nicknames for each other. To Jessie's amusement, the label's legal team seized the material and began to review it with concern. "We took it to the label and they were like: 'What is this?'" Jessie continued. "They took it straight to the legal team and I was like: 'It's nothing that dodgy!'"

While their joke sessions had been very public, there was also a secret, unreleased part of the track where the three had simply been having fun. "We actually had [the verse] 'Coconut man, call me strong, strong, strong, Jessie J got a white bum, bum, bum, Claude massive head like a moon, moon, moon!'" she laughed.

The 'Price Tag' collaboration had marked the end of a very successful set of recording sessions with Dr. Luke and Claude Kelly. Within just a week, Jessie had penned four hits – 'Nobody's Perfect', 'Abracadabra', 'Party In The USA' and of course 'Price Tag'.

Luke had some warm words of praise for her as a parting shot. "In terms of, like, vocal gymnastics and just, the ability of the muscle of the vocal chords and, you know, range and stuff like that, I don't think there's anyone else singing like that right now," he told VEVO.

Yet the best praise was yet to come. Excited by the videos he'd seen of her on YouTube – the very same videos she'd been advised not to put up – Jessie had attracted the attention of none other than world famous singer Justin Timberlake. On the strength of the amateur picture, shot with a cheap hand-held camcorder in front of her bathroom mirror, he'd got in touch to set up a studio session with her. He might have been a multimillion-selling recording artist, and voted in numerous polls as the best-looking man in the world, but Jessie was untroubled. "It was obviously a huge compliment, but I aspire to get to the same level as someone like that with my art, so it didn't faze me," she told *The Observer* casually. "In these situations I want to make it feel like they're meeting me as much as I'm meeting them – in a nice way!"

In fact, she was so keen to keep up the demeanour of ice-cold nonchalance, that when she first came face to face with him, she pretended that she didn't know his name. "I went in and I was like: 'Hi, what's your name?' and everyone was like: 'Is she joking?'" Jessie recalled to The Celeb Factory. "But I didn't want him to think I know everything about him just because he's famous."

She certainly wasn't playing the role of a starstruck teenager and perhaps it was a refreshing change for Justin, who had been a long-time target for the type of teenage fans who'd scream hysterically on meeting him, or cry so hard they could barely breathe. Jessie might have been playing it cool in comparison, but she still took the time to listen to his advice on surviving the industry. "He said: 'Make sure you play this to win, don't do it for the fame or success, do it because you love it and want to make a change' – and that's how I've always lived my career," she mused. He also advised Jessie to "roll the punches", never to let anyone pull her down and to maintain a good work ethic.

Jessie was about to learn first-hand just how strong Justin's own was, when they spent a week together, jamming in the studio. "When he's in the studio, he's in the studio," Jessie exclaimed to *Glamour*. "We would literally spend 14 hours in there and not leave. I would be like: 'Where is the toilet, please? I'm going to wet myself!'... Someone like him, they're in for a good 12 hours before they eat or even think about going out to see daylight again."

While she was recovering from the exhaustion of such rabid ambition, Justin dropped a bombshell – that he thought she was the best singer in the world. "Justin sat me down and said: 'You have the most incredible voice I've ever heard.' When someone says that to you, you want to do one of those dance moves and sing: 'Love and sex and magic!'" she joked.

Not so cool and calm after all! However, Jessie was so focused on success that his words didn't even give her an ego boost. Instead of becoming complacent, she simply piled the pressure on herself. "It's like getting an A-star in your first exam when you're four years old and then panicking," she revealed. "Now I have to revise for everything."

While the sessions with Justin hadn't resulted in any tracks to be used on her debut album, it had been valuable experience for Jessie, and she left confident that the two would work together again.

There were more celebrity collaborations in store for her soon after when she wrote a song with Chris Brown, 'I Need This', for his 2009 album *Graffiti*. Talking of needing space to breathe away from a much-loved yet possessive partner, it was thematically similar to one of Chris' previous tracks, 'Air'. Yet, while the latter was about not being able to breathe when separated from a lover, Jessie's version was about losing her breath when her lover was too close. She'd ended up liking the track so much that she decided to record a version for her own album, too. Jessie also took up an invitation to record two songs, 'I Owe It All To You' and 'Move', for Dutch *X Factor* winner Lisa Lois for her album, *Smoke*.

However, above all, she was focusing on her own debut. She'd updated 'Sexy Silk' to create an equally jazzy track with a burlesque vibe called 'Mama Knows Best'. It was an ode to the ever-supportive parents she had dubbed her "two best friends". "My mum and dad always know best," Jessie confessed. "I hate to admit that sometimes but the song says it all."

Jessie also revisited the first song she ever wrote, 'Big White Room', to try to find a way to perfect it. It was important for her to do it justice because it was her way of celebrating her young wardmate who'd died when she was 11.

After nine frustrating attempts to record a perfectly polished studio version, she gave up, deciding it would be more authentic if it was recorded live. "There's something about it that every time I recorded it in the studio, it didn't feel right," Jessie told *YRB*. "It felt like something was suffocating me and I couldn't do it. It was hard. I recorded it about nine times and we tried to produce it, but it didn't work and I was just like: 'This song is so personal and so much about the performance and melody and atmosphere, why can't we just do it live'. So we did – and it worked."

She added: "I just wanted it to almost feel like I was singing it to him with everyone listening. I'd like to think, and I hope and pray, he's in a better place and not in pain any more. The beauty of music is he lives on."

It was a painful and poignant moment for Jessie herself as, in her childhood, her heart condition had been touch and go and his fate could just as easily have been her own.

She then began work on 'Stand Up', a stomping reggae tune filled with the mantras that Jessie had adopted as a guide for life since the onset of her health problems. This was no self-help gimmick. In fact, the lyrics had meant so much to her that she'd had them tattooed on her inner right arm. "Every lyric in that song is what I live by," she asserted. "You have to stand up for what you believe in. When you're 22 and you've got the whole world at your feet, you have to just go for it. Life isn't guaranteed, so go for it, believe in yourself and make mistakes – that's what life's about."

Meanwhile, 'Who's Laughing Now' was dedicated to naming and shaming people in her past and their attempts at faux friendship. With hints of hip-hop artists like Lady Sovereign, the sound resembled her track '9 To 5' with a soul diva chorus added on. Meanwhile, the theme of near strangers turning up and showering her with false sentiments when she began to hit the big time echoed N-Dubz's track 'Feva Las Vegas'.

Using her father's self-help mantra, 'Laughter is the best therapy', Jessie also injected a slice of humour into her track to rival the wit of both songs and to make the best of a bad situation. It was a shout-out to fake friends, telling them they were fooling nobody. She was hitting out at ex-classmates she barely knew who tried to cosy up to her on social networking sites once they learned she was in LA and had a record deal. "I don't base friendship on knowing someone for five minutes in my past," she dismissed.

She was also out for the blood of the bullies she'd suffered as a teenager, those who'd gone as far as throwing rocks at her face, who now wanted to build bridges and compliment her on her voice, not mentioning their past history with her. "It's funny how people rewrite history when it suits them," she claimed. "It doesn't mean those days when you've pulled my hair or called me names have disappeared. I wanted to write a song about it, but in an uplifting way."

She added to *Times Of India*: "The song is to all those people, my music teacher or the guy that never believed in me. All the teachers that would tell me to shut up and all the kids who bullied me. People that would not be very nice to me and not really like my music and all of a sudden, when I was doing well, they would creep out and want to come to gigs and pretend to be my best friends. That's what this song is about, all the people who didn't believe – the non-believers." As an empowerment track, it was the ultimate slap in the face to the bullies who had transformed into groupies overnight and become desperate to win her favour.

Another empowerment song she'd worked on had been 'Do It Like A Dude', her answer to the "oppressive male egos" in her life. Jessie could do it like them any day she wanted, and she wasn't about to be belittled, downtrodden or silenced. Sometimes a song was all that was needed to cheer her up and to show her strength both to herself and those who tried to sap it. 'Do It Like A Dude' and 'Who's Laughing Now', both co-written by production team The Invisible Men, were testament to that.

Another subject that Jessie had wanted to cover was her struggle with her sexuality. While her parents and sisters had been supportive, jokingly dubbing her a "hardcore rebel", it hadn't been as easy to win everyone's support. 'Casualty Of Love' was her answer to Amy Winehouse's 'Some Unholy War', a defiant promise to fight for the person she loves and, more importantly, her right to love them freely against a backdrop of prejudice.

The song had been inspired musically by R&B classics of the nineties such as Mariah Carey's 'Fantasy', TLC's 'Waterfalls', '7 Days' by Craig David, '2 Become 1' by The Spice Girls and Mariah's entire *Unplugged* album. However, unlike all of these, Jessie's was no insipid love song about a heterosexual couple. "It was all about my sexuality and feeling like I had to fight to be like: 'This is who I am and if I love someone, I'm gonna go down until the last round and be a casualty of love,'" she claimed in a video interview with the record company. "I think a lot of people fight for love."

'L.O.V.E.' was another song about Jessie's sexuality, featuring a refrain where the word is spelled out that mimicked the "ella"s in Rihanna's 'Umbrella'. Realising she'd fallen head over heels for Kira, she'd originally wanted to write her a private love song. Terrified that she'd be typecast as just another Katy Perry exploiting male fantasies of two girls together to make herself a millionaire, she'd been reluctant to play the song to anyone but her team.

"I went into the studio and said: 'I wanna write a song about someone I'm in love with but I don't want anyone to hear it cuz it was one of my first serious relationships with a girl and I was so in love with her and I just wanted to write a song about it," Jessie explained. "I didn't want it to become a gimmick, I didn't want to use my sexuality as something like: 'Okay, this is with a girl' and I didn't want the label to hear it."

128

While she was adamant that she had recorded a private love song, she was eventually persuaded to consider selling it to someone else, therefore removing all association with herself from the equation. She sent it to Mary J. Blige, who politely rejected it, as did Christina Aguilera. Alicia Keys was interested and even recorded it, but she ultimately had to give it up after falling pregnant and putting her album plans on hold. "I thought: 'You know what? There's a reason this song keeps coming back to me!'" Jessie exclaimed.

Following on from that moment of realisation, she made it her mission to use it herself. It had broken the promises she'd made to herself never to write a song about love and she even found herself blushing bright red when she tried to sing it in the early days, a track she affectionately referred to as her "wedding song".

She realised she might already have an album, but something was missing. "I wanted the perfect song to glue all the other songs together – one song that sums up every single thing I've gone through," she vowed.

However, she didn't find that elusive all-encompassing track until her recording sessions had almost ended. She was exhausted, emotionally drained and couldn't wait to go home, but ironically, her misery sparked the inspiration of that perfect final track she'd been waiting for.

"I was just like: 'I don't know who I am any more,'" Jessie told *I Like Music.* "I've been shoved around a thousand different studios, I've written over six hundred songs for my debut album and I've had to whittle it down to 14 – I don't think I've got any melodies left."

Even worse, Jessie was falling prey to an inferiority complex. She was constantly exposed to women with porcelain white teeth and perfect smiles, size zero skin-tight jeans and a face full of surgical enhancements. Jessie, on the other hand, had a bob haircut that she herself described as "a cross between Mystic Meg and Lego Man", while many of the women she'd met in LA had long blonde hair down to their waists. It was also the cosmetic surgery capital of the world, and those involved in the dark world of showbiz were even more focused on perfection than everyone else.

Against this backdrop, Jessie couldn't handle her flaws. Suddenly, she felt exposed and self-conscious, under pressure to become like the others if she wanted to succeed. "I was by myself and so confused," Jessie confessed to *Flavour* in memory of the moment. "I didn't know who I was any more. I was being shoved around from labels to studios... I'd just given up being on stage. I looked in the mirror and one bit of hair wasn't in place. I remember getting so angry because this one hair wasn't perfect and I just began to cry."

Desperate for a shoulder to cry on in a world where every face seemed competitive and hostile, Jessie phoned her mother for a chat. "I was talking about all these crazy women I'd met in LA who were so different from me," she recalled. "I was really down on that day. I was trying to remember who I was before I went out and was surrounded by all these women who were so Hollywood perfect on the outside."

The following day, Jessie walked back into the studio to conquer her fears and ended up singing a track through tears, emotion spilling out. "The day I wrote it, I would've rather been in Essex eating pie and mash and watching an old episode of *One Foot In The Grave*," she continued. "The words just fell out of me. It was exactly what I wanted to say about myself when I was that lost."

It was validating for Jessie to be able to profit from her pain by turning it into a song, 'Who You Are'. She was defiant about not leaving who she was on "the shelf" in a quest to become the next blonde model singled out for Hollywood stardom – being who she was could be something that made her unique and set her apart from the perfect crowd, perhaps in a good way. Determined to remember to be herself at all costs, after the recording, Jessie visited a tattoo parlour to get the words "don't lose who you are in the blur of the stars" imprinted across her hip. She carefully copied out the phrase for her tattooist to ink but, when his work was done, she had a heart-lurching shock – she'd spelt it wrong and the word "lose" had accidentally become "loose". "My mum cried!" Jessie admitted to *Q*. "Typical me."

Even her tattoo wasn't perfect, but perhaps the experience was trying to tell her something. Maybe nobody was perfect, but she could always rely on being who she was. "That song saved my life," Jessie added. "Literally."

Chapter 7

Spikes, Dykes And Shock Value

"Girls grabbing their dicks? What's wrong with that?"

Jessie J

Fast forward a few months in time and a few thousand miles east to a Romford bedroom in the early hours of one August morning, when the glow from Jessie's mobile phone lit up the darkness. She might have cursed the unwelcome wake-up call as she wiped the sleep from her eyes – but, with that phone call, news was about to break that would change her life forever.

Up until then, it had been years of hard graft and two failed attempts at fame. Gaining a new record deal had been heartening, but Jessie still wasn't ready to believe success would really happen for her until she saw one of her songs hit the charts. So far, she hadn't been blessed with any tangible sign of success and it was only the fans on YouTube that had kept her going. But now she was about to receive the proof that, beyond all doubt, the public loved her songs – 'Party In The USA' had just hit number one.

Her first reaction was disbelief. "I think being a songwriter at 21 and having a number one hit in the US when you're from London is kind of unknown," Jessie told Neon Limelight. "It felt amazing when they called me and I was like: 'Yeah, whatever!' And they're like: 'No, really!' I was like: 'Oh, wow! The pressure's on now!'"

Jessie was about to have another moment of pride when she first heard the track air on radio – of all places, in the furniture store Ikea. "I went into Ikea when it was playing and I was like: 'I know this song!' while I was picking up, like, a dustbin," she joked to The Celeb Factory. "And you know when it's like, no one cares... but not many people can say they've written a number one in the USA at 21."

According to Jessie, most people were too busy arguing over which furnishings to buy to pay attention to her tune, but Miley Cyrus' team had snapped it up. Miley had released it as the lead single from the EP *The Time Of Our Lives*, which hit shops on August 28, 2009. It had quickly become a commercial success story, reaching the Top 10 in eight countries and selling nearly five million copies in the States alone. It would be Miley's highest-charting single of her career so far, hitting triple-platinum status in America and becoming the best-selling and fastest-selling track her label, Hollywood Records, had ever released. Miley also became the youngest artist ever to sell more than 4 million downloads of her song – yet, ironically, Jessie when she wrote the song had been even younger!

The song was a record-breaker in so many ways – and it had come from a 21-year-old British girl without a previous formal writing credit to her name. As if that wasn't enough, could Jessie have been credited with giving a then mousy Miley an image and attitude overhaul too?

At first glance, the similarities between Miley and Jessie seemed few and far between. They both shared the anguish of a mild heart condition, which caused the two episodes of accelerated heart beats, but aside from that, the pair were demonstrably different.

Miley's image couldn't have been more squeaky clean if an entire team of clergymen had been working on it - in fact, in the eyes of most Republican-voting parents, she was the ideal role model for their daughters. She had publicly promised to save her virginity until her wedding night and had boasted of how she was "brought up in a Christian family". All of this meant that Miley was a regular fixture on the child-friendly Disney Channel, where she'd been the star of the TV series *Hannah Montana*. She'd also been living in Nashville, Tennessee, where she had fitted in perfectly with its ultra-religious culture. With catchphrases like "we are all God's children", Miley seemed sweet and innocent to the core, but she was seriously lacking in R&B street cred. That was where Jessie had been able to help.

A sexually liberated Essex girl who might have wanted to be a role model but was still irrepressibly honest, Jessie wasn't pretending to be a goody two shoes. What was more, she was comfortable with outfits that the more conservative Miley would have baulked at. Yet, as 'Party In The USA' made waves with a wider, more mainstream and secular audience, Miley began to change just as much as her musical style. She was borrowing some of her British sister's liberated spirit.

Pioneering the song at the Teen Choice Awards, Miley showed a side of herself that had never been seen before. She wore skimpy hot pants and a top that flashed her bra to the crowd. What was more, a formerly demure Miley danced provocatively around what seemed to many to be a stripper pole. Meanwhile, in the song's video, the stage was backed by a giant stars & stripes flag, the word "USA" emblazoned above it.

Miley described the song as "all American" but to more conservative listeners, her dancing was anything but. The backlash wasn't long in coming – her actions were said to have inflamed religious sensitivities and outraged Christian values. One child psychologist took to the newspapers to rage: "She was communicating to her fans that it's acceptable to pole dance. Miley's only 16!"

What was more, Miley's biggest scandal prior to that had been posing for private and mildly provocative bikini shots that accidentally found their way into the public domain. The pictures were tame; many teenage celebrities might have been more mortified that the bright green bra peeking out was a little garish and unfashionable. So what, many surmised, if they flashed a little flesh – they were just having fun.

However, 'Party In The USA' had sparked a new era of naughtiness for Miley, who was evidently growing up fast. Soon after, she would be filmed giving a producer a lap dance at a party where drinks were flowing freely. Her father assured the press that she was merely "having fun" and doing "what people her age do".

However, he found it harder to defend her drug bust weeks later, when she was seen smoking the legal psychoactive plant salvia divinorum from a bong at her LA home. It was hardly Amy Winehouse's crack-smoking home video, but in the eyes of some, the image that had made her the face of the multibillion-dollar Disney franchise was now tarnished forever. Her clean living and promise to be a "moral teenager" had up to that point netted her almost $1 billion, but – according to Disney Channel Worldwide President Gary Marsh – there would be no second chances. "For Miley Cyrus to be a 'good girl' is now a business decision for her," he told *Portfolio* magazine. "Parents have invested in her godliness. If she violates that trust, she won't get it back."

Yet Miley was rapidly discovering that a slightly raunchy and irresistibly dangerous image might just be even more marketable than her clean-cut Christian persona – if only she knew how to flaunt it. Senior editor of *US Weekly*, Ian Drew, compared her to Britney Spears, saying: "She was the good girl gone bad and it looks to be working for Miley as well."

Miley wasn't the first preacher's daughter type to rebel and end up astride a stripper pole – Katy Perry had beaten her to that – but the wholesome image she'd strived so hard to maintain was crumbling fast. It was what the world had been waiting for: the subversion of an angel-faced teenager.

In perhaps the most controversial step of all, Miley then followed Jessie's lead by challenging the values of her traditional Christian upbringing, which preached that same-sex love was a sin. In a tweet to openly gay blogger Perez Hilton, she contested: "God's greatest commandment is to love – and judging is not loving! I am a Christian and I love you – gay or not."

Not all Christians loved what she had to say, however. Randy Thomasson, president of the group Save California, claimed that being gay was a "sexual sin" and insisted that Miley was "in stark conflict with Jesus Christ and the Bible".

By now just 17, her life had taken an interesting turn already, and 'Party In The USA' was the soundtrack to her transformation. However, that wasn't the end of the controversy. Miley went on to publicly confess that not only was the track not to her personal taste – hastily picked as a way to promote her clothing line – but that, despite singing about vibing to a Jay-Z song, she'd never even heard one. "Honestly, I picked that song because I needed something to go with my clothing line," she had said. "I didn't write it... and I didn't expect it to be popular originally."

When she was asked which Jay-Z song had inspired her reference to the rapper and whether she was a big fan, it might have seemed a stupid question with an inevitable answer. Not so – Miley responded: "I've never heard a Jay-Z song. I don't listen to pop music. 'Party In The USA' is not even my style of music." In that case, how had the reference made it on to the CD at all, reporters questioned. Miley's response? "I didn't write the song, so I have no idea."

Jessie's song about her first writing trip to the USA had fitted well with Miley's personal situation – relocating from Tennessee to California to pursue her career – but aside from that, they clearly had little in common. According to Jessie, Miley's only contribution to the track had been to change one of the artists she did a shout-out for to Britney.

Jessie remained tight-lipped about how Miley's less than subtle comments regarding her indifference to the song and her astonishment when it turned out to be popular had made her feel. However, she had later sneered at those who didn't write their own music. "Songwriting is a big product of me wanting to be a solo artist that has control over what they do," she later told *This Is Essex*. "There are a lot of artists out there who are just dummies, getting dressed by management, being told what to say and sing and wear, but I'm really proud of the fact that I write songs."

Yet Miley was one of the pop star puppets she'd been speaking of – someone who admitted she had no idea what her signature tunes were about or where the ideas for them came from. Were her comments a subtle slap in the face for Miley?

Regardless of the politics, Jessie was thrilled at the news of her first number one, talking gleefully of wanting to give Miley a "high five" and joking that the song would be paying her rent for some time to come.

However, the cash injection into Jessie's career didn't numb her ambitions – her main motivation had never been money. She'd set herself an almost impossibly high standard with her number one and now she had to make her own material live up to that too. "I'm trying to top it every day," she told Neon Limelight.

The news of her success even reached Britney Spears, whose management sent her a beat that would be the star's next single and asked her to write a winning song over it. Meanwhile Jessie's early track, 'Sexy Silk', which had never been formally released, was purchased for a film called *Easy A* – also known as *Easy Girl* – about promiscuity.

The film, featuring *Friends* star Lisa Kudrow, was set in an American high school where reputation is all important. In it, the school nerd (Olive, played by Emma Stone) becomes an unlikely prostitute, without so much as dropping her pants. It all begins when, vying for attention with the more popular girls in her class, she tells a little white lie about a weekend of sex with a university student several years older. Relishing the attention, she devises a way to both boost her bank account and secure instant popularity – by accepting money to pretend she's had sex. First she strikes a bargain with a gay classmate desperate to hide his secret and maintain the pretence of being straight. Then she seals the deal with straight boys desperate to improve their social standing by being able to boast of another notch on their bedposts.

However, news of her faux bed-hopping soon reaches the local church group, who launch a campaign to get her expelled from school. Things become even worse when her best friend's boyfriend uses her as a fake scapegoat when he contracts an STI. It turns out that he cheated on his girlfriend with a school teacher, but Olive agrees to take the blame to save the teacher's skin.

As the situation becomes more and more out of hand, revolted classmates are reluctant to date her, fearing that she has an infection but little knowing that in reality she is still a virgin.

The last straw comes when she has to fend off the advances of a would-be rapist who thinks his financial gift will buy him more than just the rumour that they slept together. Realising she wants to come clean and end the illusions, she confesses all and ends up dating her long-time crush – and remains a virgin even as the film ends.

Despite their very different circumstances, there were a few parallels between Jessie and Olive. Jessie too had once been the school nerd that no one wanted to hang out with, who'd later experienced a sudden surge in popularity after she'd made it among classmates who'd shunned her so much at school that they were virtual strangers. Jessie had also experienced the perils of the rumour mill first-hand, feeling the need to write a song to apologise. Incidentally, Olive's confession at the end of the film is told through a song too. Finally, she and Olive share an obsession with music to get through the tough times. When a lonely Olive is pretending to spend the weekend with a boyfriend, in reality she is staying at home, repeatedly singing 'Pocketful Of Sunshine' by Natasha Bedingfield to while away the hours.

The film made its debut on October 22, while Jessie's song was chosen for an accompanying Nivea campaign. "I remember seeing the ad at the cinema and wanting to tell everyone: 'That's me! That's me!'" she recalled.

Once the euphoria of her public exposure had worn off, she started a stint of promotional activities to make sure it wasn't a flash in the pan. On the same day as the film release, she performed live on the runway for the opening of the *Britain's Next Top Model* live show in London. Jessie herself had just been taken on by a fashion agency called Next Models, which not only had artists like Kelis, Pharrell Williams and Professor Green on its books, but also catered for catwalk supermodels such as the six-foot-tall Brazilian fashionista Ana Beatriz-Barros.

Jessie's networking at the show itself saw her meet Tyra Banks, who later joked: "Fierce Jessie J... wanted me to tell her she was in the running to be America's next top model." In fact, Jessie had even been practising her walk for the occasion.

As well as meeting her idols, she performed in every single catwalk show across the three-day event. While that had been the show that formally launched Jessie's solo career, she was also due to perform new showcases in the USA. On November 2, she played five songs at LA's Stone Rose nightclub – 'Mamma Knows Best', 'Who You Are', 'Stand Up', 'Price Tag' and 'L.O.V.E.'. She arrived in a boyish baseball cap and a plain black vest top, presenting herself as the antithesis of America's obsession with perfection. Yet she received glowing praise.

Artistdirect raved: "The crowd wasn't simply privy to new tunes from the buzzing English artist – they got a taste of pop's future and it's a very sweet one at that." The site claimed that she was "unpredictable musically and that's where Jessie's brilliance lies", calling all five tunes "instant classics". Commenting on her heartfelt intro to 'Who You Are', where she confessed that she had once "lost myself" in the search for fame, the website added: "Jessie J deserves to be one of the biggest stars in the world because she's not afraid to be who she is."

According to Arjan Writes, a blog aimed at music industry insiders, tweets across the internet had revealed people that were "unanimously, completely, utterly and totally impressed".

What was more, LA blogger Winston Ford, who was reportedly recognised as "an international music tastemaker by industry insiders and musicians in the know", was equally enamoured by Jessie. "I love discovering new talent and I'm always excited about judging new voices like it's my personal *American Idol*," he said. "I used to spend hours trying to find the next big thing, but this era of media over-saturation, it seems like finding a true singer is becoming that digital media in the haystack. There are few people that stand out. Jessica Cornish is that girl. Forget Auto-Tune and slick production – this is pure, raw talent."

It was glowing praise, and all before she'd so much as played a single song to the general public. If the so-called taste-makers were to be believed, Jessie was just what America was looking for, and cracking a country so much bigger than her own might not be that elusive after all.

In spite of that, Jessie was keen to start out on home territory and was so desperate to release her song in England first that she'd "begged" the record label to listen. "I grew up watching *Top Of The Pops* and always wanted to be a part of the British music scene," she told *Closer*, leaving no doubt about where her loyalties lay. "I begged my American label: 'Please let me release in the UK first!'"

Fortunately for her, it made a good business decision too – and they instantly agreed. "It made sense to have the UK take the lead because she lives there and things can happen so quickly over there," Jason Flom explained. "In the UK, BBC Radio 1 is dominant nationally and their support gives you a lot of recognition overnight, whereas in the US you have to go one station at a time and you build in many different ways. England is also a much smaller country but still has influence in the US – the taste-makers over there have an impact on what happens here.

"Instead of launching simultaneously and having to split Jessie's time back and forth between the two countries, it made more sense for her to stay over there for a few months to break the market. Island were so excited about Jessie from the beginning and have such an incredible hot streak right now with Mumford and Sons and Florence and the Machine that it just made sense to us to have Jessie released there initially."

While that meant Jessie wouldn't be spending most of her waking hours flitting from airport to airport, it didn't mean that she lacked potential stateside. "This is not a sprint, it's a marathon," Jason continued. "We see her as an important artist in the long term. I think the US is going to be a huge market for her."

Jessie duly returned to the UK and, on November 9, made her first live TV debut with an acoustic performance of 'Price Tag' on *Later With Jools Holland*. Beamed out to millions of households on BBC2, it was bound to have an impact, but there was one supporter Jessie hadn't been expecting: Kylie Minogue. Taking to her Twitter account, the Australian starlet showered her with praise, claiming: "Jessie J is SOSOSOSOSO amazing! Check her out."

While she felt a rush of pride, Jessie wasn't about to get complacent. Kylie's comments would elevate would-be fans' expectations, so she had only raised the bar higher. "You don't go: 'Wow, thank you!'" she told *The Guardian*. "You think: 'Right, I've got something to prove now.'"

Indeed she did – with the release of her first single, 'Do It Like A Dude'. The song was a hard-hitting, attention-grabbing parody of macho hip-hop culture, and her bid to release some oestrogen into the charts. "At the time I felt the chart was very Auto-Tune heavy," Jessie told *Contactmusic*. "There were a lot of guys with their trousers down by their knees and their neck chains so heavy they couldn't hold their heads up."

It wasn't just in the charts – Jessie was seeing the very same situation unfold in the studio with her production team, The Invisible Men. Bored in the studio, Jessie took to the mic and began to poke fun at their clothes, to her, the embodiment of a negative hip-hop scene. "I was bored with the song I was writing and there were two boys – two producers called Parker and James – and one of them wears his trousers ridiculously low," Jessie added to *PrideSource*. "So I just started freestyling!"

First she started taunting: "If we had to run for the bus, you'd never make it" but then turned her jokes into full-on singing – and within 15 minutes, they'd got a hit.

It might have been a joke song that had taken just a quarter of an hour to perfect, but the tune also had a deeper meaning. It came at a time when gangsta rap was growing in popularity, an era which saw artists such as Pitbull accused of womanising. Yet it had become an acceptable norm for the genre. Women were the artists' "bitches" and the more the latter could brag about conquering, the more notches they could display on their bedposts, the cooler they were according to the rules of hip-hop culture. Music videos often showed a single man surrounded by a dozen or so beauties who seemed to serve no other purpose than to shake their booties obligingly and serve some chilled champagne. The lifestyle became a must-have icon of power and social supremacy. Anyone who was anyone in the hip-hop game had a woman in every town and probably more. To Jessie, hip hop had become as much a token of misogyny as the football world.

Moreover, perhaps it didn't help that when singers made it big, they found themselves surrounded by groupies, many of whom would be clamouring to spend the night with them. Enamoured by the fame and the luxurious lifestyle, some women threw themselves at the stars, perpetuating the hip-hop myth.

Yet Jessie took exception to the notion of women as possessions, as much a symbol of status as a new Mercedes or a mansion with a built-in cinema. For these people, she felt, a hot girl on their arm was a sign that they'd finally made it. "There's some people coming back around and bringing hip hop back, but I feel like too much is about bitches and hoes and chains and cars and how many girls are naked," she told Clayton Perry.

She also wanted to point out the double standards that she felt still existed – that men could sleep around and earn respect for being a cheeky "Jack the lad", but if women did the same, their reputation was tarnished and they were branded whores. "Guys sleep around and say they've got this and that and cars and girls [but] if it were girls who were doing that, it's a totally different story," Jessie added.

However, there was more to Jessie's hit-back anthems than a proclamation that she could do all of the same things – there was a more personal meaning to it. "I've had a lot of male egos in my life that have made me feel like I can't do things as well as them or they're more powerful than me," she revealed to *Times Of India.* "Not just physically but you have to emotionally feel like: 'You know what? I can get up in front of 10,000 people and make a speech on national TV' and you have to be able to do it. You don't get training for it, you just have to have the confidence to do it."

Therefore the song was on one hand a "tongue in cheek parody of a stereotypical male", but it was also an ode to the men in Jessie's own life who had tried to oppress her or knock down her confidence.

What was more, it had an empowerment message – it wasn't just about being able to urinate standing up without soaking the toilet seat. "The deeper meaning is that everyone is equal," she told Global Grind. "No one should make you feel intimidated and you can go: 'You know what, eff you, I can be who I wanna be and stand on my own two feet and not feel like I can't because you're making me feel like I can't... It's not that I hate men. It's not like we're saying: 'Women are better, we hate men.' That's not it at all. But you know, sometimes it's nice to have an empowered feeling that makes everybody so equal."

The song was perfect for Jessie, but her first hit had almost passed her by altogether: she'd been about to send it to Rihanna. That was, of course, until mutual friend Justin Timberlake urged her to keep it for herself, and her label felt the same way. "I wrote it with Rihanna in mind because 'Rude Boy' was out at the time and that's kinda what inspired me to write the song," she revealed to Rap-Up. "At first I never really saw myself doing something like it, but I knew I could. I sent it to my label and I was like: 'I'm just sending you this before I send it to Rihanna's camp to see if you guys like it.' And they were like: 'This is your first single. It's amazing.'"

"Sorry, Rihanna!" Jessie joked, formally taking on the track for herself. On the day of the video shoot, she did pay tribute to Rihanna and what could have been when she donned some spiky shoulder pads, just as her American counterpart had done for the song 'Hard'. Meanwhile, the location of the shoot was thought by the public to be a lesbian bar or prison but, in reality, Jessie was getting down and dirty in the basement of a church. It seemed slightly inappropriate, echoing the time she'd stood out for wearing a leather fetish outfit for a day of mourning on the Don't Trigger campaign's showcase. However, this time Jessie did feel a little self-conscious. "I feel really weird dressed like this in a church," she joked on set.

The video might have been filmed in a place of worship, but it portrayed a women's-only underground club where – in the explicit version – two girls intimately kissed. She'd outdone Katy Perry on her very first video. A more strait-laced Katy had refused to entertain the idea of sapphic kissing on her own video for 'I Kissed A Girl', claiming she didn't want her work to be turned into a "freak show parade". She was singing about locking lips with a woman but sneering at the idea of it actually happening – or was Katy calling herself a freak?

While the public might have been confused, with Jessie there was no such ambiguity. To add to the vibe of a lesbian bar, her girlfriend, Kira, also appeared in the video – a boyish-looking mixed-race girl with a caramel-brown skin tone and a short hairstyle.

It was a comedy parody of the crotch-grabbing male and his outer misogyny, even displaying the women ridiculing stereotypically macho images like cutting into a piece of meat. This was no pastel-coloured girly-girl video – and for Jessie, it was just as well. "[Skirts and dresses have] never been my thing," she confided to Global Grind, "because I'm so out there. I feel uncomfortable and I can't move."

To counter the image that she was a passive, available woman, Jessie's lips were painted jet black and adorned with spikes – anyone who thought this girl was available or up for a gentle kiss would get an unwelcome shock.

Jessie toned down the video for TV, providing both an explicit tape for post-watershed viewers and a clean version for during the day. In both, the message was simple: women could not be defeated.

The explicit version hit the music channels on November 9, while its tamer sidekick reached 4Music a day later, both sporting the trademark spiked lips, of course.

The first reaction for many was shock, especially for those who had known Jessie in her schooldays. "That video was all drugs and lesbians and I was like: 'Jess doesn't even do caffeine!'" BRIT School classmate Kerry Louise Barnaby exclaimed to the author.

The world was soon rushing to download it and find out who this man-bashing, lesbian-loving hard girl really was – and the song's success exceeded all of Jessie's expectations. "I was hoping it would get to 10,000 hits in a week [on YouTube] and it was at 2 million in that time," she revealed to the *Daily Record*. "I was like: 'Okay. If more people want to watch it, that's all right.' The internet is so global that as soon as something is put on it, it's there for the whole world. I can track where people are watching most. It's really big in South America, Japan and Poland and even now I'm being played on Jamaican radio!"

It was hardly surprising that Jessie had endeared herself to Caribbean audiences with her use of their traditional street talk. However, for those who hadn't grown up with American slang or Jamaican culture around them, the song might have needed a little more translation, and, in interviews with the media, Jessie was only too happy to oblige. "Man'dem is a street term here in the UK for, like, the boys, like a group of boys – 'Oh, it's me and the man'dem!'" Jessie explained to Clayton Perry. "I've grown up with a lot of different cultures around me."

There were also countless interpretations of Jessie's demand to get her dollar licked. Some thought that it was a hint at prostitution, while others felt she was asking men to bow down to her economic self-reliance. If the latter was the case, she'd be attempting feminism, Destiny's Child's 'Independent Women' style. However, Jessie soon cleared up the rumours in an interview with the gay magazine *PrideSource*. "It's purely when guys flash their money at the club," she laughed. "A lot of people think there's a secret meaning to it, but it's because I was initially writing the song for Rihanna that I put the dollar thing in it. I was going to take it out because, obviously, I'm English. I would say: 'You need to lick my pound' but it doesn't really have the same vibe!"

Also, while Snoop Dogg and 50 Cent had bragged about being "pimps" with the song 'P.I.M.P.', Jessie had hit back by spelling out "B.I.T.C.H." in 'Do It Like A Dude'.

From a joke track that she'd never intended to release to a feisty number that she felt "had Rihanna's swagger all over it" to her very own first single, 'Do It Like A Dude' had come a long way. Now it had listeners in its millions. However, with a viewer count that soon exceeded 15 million on YouTube alone, it was inevitable that not everyone would warm to what seemed to be a feminist empowerment anthem.

There was a tidal wave of disapproval to accompany the praise, but Jessie was ready for the backlash and had an answer to every criticism. Her former dance tutor, Dawn Wenn-Kober, had told the author the song didn't do justice to Jessie's classically trained singing voice, implying that it relied on shouting, stomping and shock value rather than the vocal wizardry she was capable of. That was a view echoed by many listeners but, according to Jessie, she knew that already and had deliberately released the song as a calculated decision to guarantee she arrived on the music scene amid scandal and controversy. "I'm kind of fighting it when people say: 'This is not Jessie J. This is not a singer's song,'" Jessie told Clayton Perry. "I'm like: 'They do know that I know that right? I'm a businesswoman!'"

She added: "You have to be a businesswoman. You can't survive in this industry if you don't know what you're doing [and] if I had put out 'Price Tag' first on the internet globally, tried to launch with that, I think it wouldn't have got the same amount of attention that 'Do It Like A Dude' did. It shook up some controversy. I think that's what you have to do. You have to put yourself out there and go: 'I'm ready. Are you?'"

Jessie might have been ready, but some male viewers certainly weren't – in fact, they launched their own remixes to put themselves on the war path. "It's very funny how a lot of the reactions that I had and a lot of the remixes that were done, the men would attack the women and kinda go: 'You can't do it like us, we can do it better than you,'" Jessie recalled to *Onion* magazine. "[But] it's not about me hating men. Obviously as a woman you wanna feel empowered and you wanna feel confident and proud to be a woman – and I very much am. But I wanted that song to be just about experiences that I've had in my life with some male egos where you feel that they don't think that you're equal to them. It's nothing to do with women being better than men – I don't actually say that once in the song... I never said that guys don't do it better than girls or vice versa. It's just me saying: 'I can do it like you, don't try to intimidate me and make me feel uncomfortable.'"

She conceded, however, that it "definitely bruised some egos". One suspected that Jessie didn't have to think hard to come up with controversy – in fact, it seemed to follow her wherever she went.

There was more bad news in store for Jessie, however, when Lewis Bowman, singer of the indie band Chapel Club, ranted about 'Do It Like A Dude' in the *NME*, claiming that she was an insult to feminism. "She's a lesbian, she's from Essex and she co-wrote the biggest-selling single in the US last year. She sounded so interesting," mused Lewis. "But then I listened to her song. *The Guardian* [was] saying 'Do It Like A Dude' is part of a conversation about feminism... This isn't part of the conversation, this is part of a general trend in pop lately of girls trying to do something they see as mildly ironic or subversive that's actually just totally what everyone expects... people like Simone de Beauvoir, you're doing them down!"

Some might have questioned what a male author would know about the appropriation of feminism. However, Jessie wasn't about to get hung up over the negativity. For her, it was about empowerment and she was proud of it regardless. "I love the song," she argued. "It's a fun club track that you can hear your own meaning to, all day, every day."

Indeed, *Autostraddle* predicted it to be the top soundtrack for every self-respecting lesbian club in the country, "every night for the rest of the year". The website added: "Yeah, it's another pop song with insipid lyrics, but have you ever been in a lesbian club when 'I Kissed A Girl' comes on? If you have, the thumping, clangy, sexy beats of 'Do It Like A Dude' will come as a welcome respite." According to them, Katy Perry was "misappropriating bisexuality by selling it as a party trick", while there was something more authentic, and far less demeaning, about Jessie that could see lesbian listeners use her as a role model.

Take that, Katy Perry – round one to Jessie! Yet the debate about what the song really meant continued. *Autostraddle* challenged: "Many might argue that 'Do It Like A Dude' paradoxically uses men/maleness as a golden standard by which to define itself." Surely a true feminist wouldn't want to follow in a man's footsteps, the reasoning went – after all, if women were equal, why would they want to be like men?

One blogger, who called himself "undercitylights", highlighted that point when he asked: "The first question that this track raises is quite why exactly reasonably attractive women like Jessie J would want to 'Do It Like A Dude'? In the pop scene that this song so obviously belongs to, it's the females who dominate. Surely all us guys should be aspiring to 'do it like a dudette' as far as pop music goes!"

Indeed, the following year would unveil a chart scene that was almost exclusively female. At one point, nine out of the top 10 artists were women. Similarly, while female *X Factor* contestants such as Leona Lewis and Alexandra Burke soared into the charts, their male counterparts almost invariably flopped miserably, with one or two being forced to resort to singing tours of half-empty coffee shops. Jessie's life was already much, much more glamorous than that.

On the other hand, the proliferation of top-quality women in the industry could work against a female newcomer to the scene, as Jessie had already found out first-hand when she was systematically rejected, one by one, by every British record label.

It was harder for Jessie to set herself apart from the crowd with so much competition, and she hadn't wanted to join a beauty contest either. "I was getting a bit fed up with the way women have to sell themselves," Jessie later told *The Mirror*. "'Do It Like A Dude' was sticking my finger up at that. You've got to have balls and go for things, feel confident and not just be girlie. I used to go to auditions and there'd be a thousand girls that looked like me – you have to stand out."

In that case, was acting like a man her way of separating herself from the countless beautiful blondes in the music business, whose stunning looks opened doors for them before they'd sung a single note? It was a strategy that had already been adopted by her idol Rihanna, who'd prided herself on trying to be "edgy" and "different" rather than sporting "long blonde hair like every other female in the game". Her short haircuts and edgy garb might have had record company execs tearing their own hair out and moaning that this wasn't the gentle, easy-on-the-eye beach babe that they'd signed, but she was doing things her own way – and it seemed that Jessie aspired to be equally uncompromising.

Tellingly, the video for 'Do It Like A Dude' had featured two photogenic blonde women kissing. Could it be that, like the rest of the video's themes, this was a parody? Was this image illuminating the theory that feminine, traditionally beautiful women were the only type of girls allowed in a man's lesbian fantasy? That society only accepted gay women when they were catering to male desires, cavorting in front of the camera to titillate a man at the centre of a threesome, or starring – legs spread – in a pornographic video? Men seemed to accept the non-threatening version of lesbian love but to baulk at anything packaged in a different way. Was Jessie saying with the parody of the two blondes – possibly faux lesbians anyway – that she was defying norms and letting the world know that she didn't have to conform to men's standards of what was attractive?

It seemed that she was portraying a subtle comedy sketch that poked fun at what men wanted. The imagery became even more interesting during the scene when a phallic symbol is torn in half. Forget doing it like a dude – was Jessie actually doing a dude down?

Either way, the video was on every music-lover's lips that month, and when the track was formally released on November 18, it proved to be just as much of a hit as the hype had predicted. It debuted at number 25 in the UK singles chart, before eventually peaking at number two. Ironically, Jessie was beaten to the top spot by a dude – Bruno Mars – with the phallic-sounding song 'Grenade'.

If, as some said, Jessie's single was all about the emancipation of women and the emasculation of men – reinforced by the castration metaphors in the video – was a chart gender war about to begin, with Jessie at the centre? While Beyoncé had disapprovingly scorned the archetypal male in 'If I Were A Boy', telling the world that she could do a better job of the role, and Ciara had merely fantasised about "switching the roles", had Jessie taken the metaphor a step further?

Either way, with 'Do It Like A Dude', a formerly unknown Essex girl had risen out of nowhere and joined the ranks of internationally famous American stars in adding to the gender debate. Who'd have thought 15 minutes of fun in the studio could have resulted in a number two hit? The song was her battle cry, and her moment had arrived, because the world was finally listening.

Chapter 8

Not The Average Essex Girl

"People keep asking me: 'How does it feel to be on this amazing roller-coaster ride?' and I'm like: 'I'm still queuing up – I haven't even started!'"

Jessie J

"The best rumour I've ever heard about myself?" Jessie spluttered. "That my partner spat in a rapper's face for trying to talk to me!" Just days into the fame game, she had already fallen prey to the type of scandal usually reserved for longstanding celebrities.

It had been her first major UK gig, joining two other artists at the Union Chapel in Islington on November 16 to open for Paolo Nutini. To any other newcomer, the audience might have seemed formidably large, but not to Jessie – she was a seasoned hand at playing arenas several times the venue's size. However, now she was a high-profile act – someone that no one could wait to see.

The event, known as Little Noise Sessions, had been Amy Winehouse's launch pad to fame after she made her mark with first album, *Frank* – and it had played host to one of Jessie's R&B idols, Craig David, a decade earlier, for a legendary acoustic session. She didn't disappoint – according to MSN, she held punters' attention with "down to earth charm and wit [and] Nicki Minaj-esque face pulling."

By the last song, her star had risen. "'Price Tag' saw her wrap up her stint on stage with a standing ovation, reportedly the only opening act to receive one in the history of the Little Noise Sessions," the review continued. "I think It's fair to say an Urban Pop Star has been born."

However, it wasn't just the quality of her performance that would keep people talking. To some gossip mongers, being seen talking to someone translated to a love affair or a full-on marriage proposal. Plus, the next day, an unguarded comment could be reported as a full-scale brawl. Not only that, but the rumours didn't need to have any truth attached to them to bring the showbiz world to a standstill.

In this instance, chart-topping singer Example had checked out Jessie's set and tried to make conversation with her later. Yet gossip columnists alleged that sparks were flying backstage with her jealous girlfriend. The rumour mill was spinning wildly out of control and it seemed to be just an inevitable consequence of her fame. Jessie had made it clear that this rumour was a pure fabrication – but nonetheless there was no doubt that the fame game was wreaking havoc on her personal life and threatening to destroy relationships with those she loved.

Her family had tried to keep her feet firmly on the ground – when her father heard the news of her 'Do It Like A Dude' chart position, he'd merely joked: "That's funny, I just did a number two!" With grounded parents like hers, there was little chance of Jessie getting above herself, believing the pop-star myths or having spoiled diva-style tantrums.

What was more, she wasn't making any extravagant purchases to match her overnight superstar status, either. She'd bought a couple of handbags one day totalling £600 and, much to her embarrassment, had seen her credit card rejected. "My record company had stopped the transaction because they thought somebody had stolen my card," Jessie cringed to the *Daily Star*. "That's how little money I get."

Within three weeks of its release, 'Party In The USA' had hit the number one spot in six countries and 'Do It Like A Dude' was following close behind – but Jessie still had about as much purchase power as an unemployed pauper – or one of the preteen "spoiled brats" she'd served in Hamleys.

With no money and no hero worshippers around her, Jessie hadn't been able to add much helium to her ego – even if she'd wanted to. However, even for a grounded girl, success was proving difficult. She could no longer go out by herself and her face was starting to appear in the newspapers. "I'm so exhausted all the time, I was up for 24 hours the other day," she told *RWD*. "You forget to eat. I hardly see my family… my whole life has been pulled from under me."

However, one of the worst things about fame for Jessie was the rumours. It was time to redress the balance, giving fans a glimpse into who she was – a straight-talking, supremely self-confident unconventional Essex girl who couldn't care less about her image and valued her talent ahead of her looks. Above all, she wanted to show that she was normal – she didn't want to be placed on a pedestal so high that it alienated her from her fans.

She was eager to share thoughts and feelings with them and viewers were equally fascinated, lusting after a glimpse of the real her. For those who hadn't been behind the scenes during her five-year struggle to the top or followed her self-released videos on YouTube, it probably seemed she'd appeared out of nowhere. Who was Jessie J? Was she a feminist, a lesbian, a man-hater? Forget that, was she simply the hottest new act to hit music?

Right on cue, her very own fly-on-the-wall TV show launched on November 29, courtesy of Myspace, to answer those questions. *Dare Jessie J* was an online documentary over a series of several 10-minute episodes where people as high profile as Tinie Tempah and as anonymous as fans dared her to do outrageous stunts in the name of work. Meanwhile, the cameras followed her every move as she prepared herself for stardom. It was an opportunity for Jessie to have some fun in the name of art, whether dressing up as a gorilla, going on a roller-coaster or running down the beach at top speed – building up hype for her album and showing fans who she was in the process.

Jessie had taken the challenge to be herself to heart, so the first episode featured her, warts and all and without a trace of make-up, at an East London studio to prepare for her first-ever photo shoot. Within seconds, the video had switched to a different Jessie – face painted with fake lashes, smoky eyeliner and bright red lips, playing with her vampish sex appeal for the camera. Nonetheless, for those few seconds, viewers were being treated to a rare glimpse of a celebrity without make-up or cover-up, freely admitting that she was far from perfect. She wasn't a sultry stunner 24 hours a day, nor did she want to be.

Plus, unlike contemporaries such as Lady Gaga, her reality was a million miles away from the outrageous costumes of her day job. "I feel like a lot of the industry and media portray this image of what beautiful is or how you should dress or how you should look. I don't think it's healthy," she told the BBC. "In [episode one of *Dare Jessie J*], I'm doing this shot of me with no make-up, where I've just woken up. I don't think a lot of people would be comfortable enough to do that. But that's the way I look. This is who I am." She later added to *The Big Issue*: "Girls in pop are often very polished and pretty... I feel like I'm exposing a bit of realness."

The episodes showed off her fun side and showcased the type of unpretentious girl mentioned in 'Price Tag', who would rather be able to dance for hours than hobble around in high-fashion stilettos, wincing from the pain. While Jessie was shown having fun with spiked shoulder pads and leotards that left little to the imagination, she could not echo Gaga's boast that she was "never in jeans". For Jessie, the show was all about casual clothes and the uninhibited joy of, for example, seeing America for the first time. It might not have been perfectly polished, but she was putting the "reality" in reality TV.

It was also an opportunity to squeeze some normality into her heavily packed promotional schedule and to sneak some good times into her working day under the guise of hard graft. "*Dare Jessie J* was always my little plan to be able to do stuff a 22-year-old would do while I'm living my day-to-day life," she admitted to *Time Out*. "Sometimes I have to remind myself to chill out, have a Nando's, put my feet up and watch comedy. And *Dare Jessie J* was just a chance for me to act like a kid in this crazy whirlwind of my life right now. I am a dork in disguise, I love doing stupid stuff."

The disguise was ripped off in the very first episode, when viewers saw R&B group N-Dubz challenge Jessie to sing in public dressed as a gorilla.

Arms outstretched in a skin tight body suit, Jessie flaunts the British flag. LINDA BROWNLEE/CORBIS OUTLINE

Jessie takes part in a hand-printing ceremony at Planet Hollywood in New York as she prepares for her album to hit American shores. NANCY KASZERMAN/ZUMAPRESS.COM

Jessie's beamed out to millions of households on one of her first ever primetime TV appearances stateside, *The Tonight Show* in LA. Despite being completely unknown to the public, she doesn't let the nerves show. NBCUPHOTOBANK/REX FEATURES

Jessie and B.O.B. perform 'Price Tag' on *Saturday Night Live* on March 12, 2011. NBCUPHOTOBANK/REX FEATURES

An injured Jessie keeps it clean as a queen at muddy Glastonbury Festival by perching on a throne in one Wellington boot and one plaster cast. CORBIS

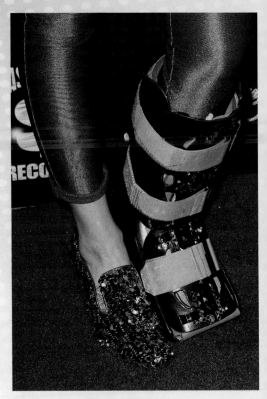

A brave Jessie hobbles to the 2011 MTV VMAs with the help of her crutches. RD/ORCHON/RETNA DIGITAL

Who says a broken foot can't be glamorous? In her second shoe change of the day, Jessie attends Lil Wayne's album launch party in LA wearing a bejewelled slipper Michael Jackson style. DAVID LIVINGSTON/GETTY IMAGES

Jessie reclines on stage at the V Festival in a stroke of Amy Winehouse inspired eyeliner as a shout out to her departed idol.
SHIRLAINE FORREST/GETTY IMAGES

backstage shot at MTV's EMAs on November 6, 2011. DAVE HOGAN/MTV 2011/GETTY IMAGES

Jessie takes to the stage at Paris's VIP room on September 21, 2011. CORBIS

Jessie dresses up as a "sad clown" complete with eyeliner tears in Leeds on October 30, 2011. EDWARD FIELDING

Jessie continues the UK tour, taking to the stage at the Manchester Apollo on October 21, 2011. SHIRLAINE FORREST/WIREIMAGE

Jessie dons some eye jewels for a sell-out concert at the Brighton Centre on November 3, 2011. MICHAEL BURNELL/REDFERNS

Undaunted by her first dare, she hailed a black cab to London's Trafalgar Square and broke into song. Unafraid of looking stupid, she screamed: "This is my gorilla gig!" to the amusement and, at times, confusion of a myriad of tourists. Some sniggered, some swerved away, others point blank ignored her – but, undeterred, Jessie had just completed her first dare.

When she wasn't taking up the challenge of smothering her vocal cords in a furry gorilla costume on a hot summer's day, she was showing her early morning make-up-free face to the cameras. "I look about 10 because my eyelashes are blonde, so I look like I've got an awful wig on," Jessie joked to the BBC. She laughed off the media scandal her bare face could cause by joking: "Do you seriously think I wake up looking like this [in full make-up]?"

The second episode saw Jessie on a promotional trip to California, taking some time out to run down Venice Beach. Despite never having done a public gig in the USA, she was soon sighted by a group of five starstruck locals, who whispered: "It's that girl, that Jessie J girl! 'Big White Room'!"

She then obligingly belted out a rendition of the song for them in the middle of the street. "It was a really inspirational moment to know I have fans on the other side of the world!" she beamed to the camera later. "Jessie J is becoming international!"

Episode two also saw Perez Hilton, the celebrity blogger the stars loved to hate, challenging Jessie to sing a cover of Travis Garland's song 'Believe' inside a cave – not the ideal dare for a girl who was both claustrophobic and scared of the dark. "Oh, Perez, I thought we were friends!" groaned Jessie. "Our friendship is over – before it even started!"

Yet, after taking just a day to learn the previously unheard track, she was ready for the dare. "He made me go into the caves where Batman used to go in the original TV show," she recalled to the BBC. "I put my own twist on it and dressed up as Batgirl."

For episode three meanwhile, she was dared by B.o.B to go to James Brown's Hollywood star in LA and do her best impression of the icon. For Jessie, the biggest problem wasn't her nerves, but the total indifference of passers-by. She implored one to dance with her, only for him to laugh and walk away without a word. "I was nervous about it, but no one was even watching," Jessie lamented later. "The dare was really fun, but no one cared!"

By episode four, she'd moved on to Nevada, where she was taking a trip to the depths of the desert – and Jessie was keen to evoke an eerie atmosphere. "Outside this car, it isn't people in houses – no, no, no," she asserted. "It's just sound – sound and little bush-snakes... and probably dead bodies!" Camped out in Death Valley, Jessie then started to tell ghost stories, which fell flat after she punctuated each sentence with hysterical laughter. Not only that, but the loud knock at the door in the dead of night was nothing more than "a man with a camera".

Jessie then moved on to the Las Vegas strip, admiring the candy-coloured Fantasy Land hotels and their larger-than-life gambling joints, before fulfilling a dare to sing nursery rhymes while a roller-coaster plunged her upside down.

An even more inventive dare was in store in episode five, when Jessie proved she wasn't afraid to make herself look silly in the name of art. Her peaceful boat trip to see New York's Statue of Liberty was interrupted by a mischievous message from Tinie Tempah, who dared her to go to the top of the steps at Times Square and break into song in front of thousands of people. At first, Jessie wasn't amused. "That's gonna be so embarrassing because there's like five million people sitting on them steps all the time!" Jessie moaned of the crowded tourist attraction. "I'm gonna lose all my dignity on this trip – but it's gonna be well worth it!"

Not only that, but she would be gracing the same location that Jay-Z and Alicia Keys had visited to film the video for 'Empire State Of Mind'. Dressed in a bright green Statue of Liberty hat, Jessie plucked up the courage to sing, surrounded by tourists. One girl, talking into her mobile phone, frowned and shook her head in disapproval, while some ignored her altogether – and with Jessie's vocal cords, she wasn't easy to ignore.

However, in spite of the knockbacks, she didn't regret what she was doing. It was an unpretentious way for her to show her fun side to fans, as well as her admirable lack of inhibitions.

Jessie came back down to earth with a bang for episode six. No longer living it up in the States, she was back on home turf to play a show, performing a rap about being frightened in Brighton in honour of it. Now it was Jessie's chance to balance out the celebrity dare contributions with some direct input from her fans. "[Celebrity input] is cool, of course it is, but I want everyone to get involved," she'd told *YRB*. "Just because someone's famous doesn't make them more important."

Thus it was a Brighton-based fan who issued Jessie with her next challenge – to sing 'Price Tag' dressed entirely in clothes from members of the audience. On imparting this news, dozens of fashion items filled the stage. Jessie rejected a pair of heels, cackling: "I'm a size 7, babe, I ain't getting in there", but everything else was accepted. She then had a moment of truth when she glanced at her reflection – by now donning a bright pink scarf, a leopard-print top and a hat with a skull on the front. "I just caught myself in the mirror – I could either be a complete loony or Lady Gaga!" Jessie laughed. "Either one!"

The next episode saw Jessie receive a dare live on a Manchester radio show that involved stuffing her mouth full of Ferrero Rocher chocolates. In a world of anorexia and self-restraint that many blamed on the influence of picture-perfect size-zero clothes, Jessie's fearless gluttony stood out a mile. Not only was she being who she was, but some might say she was setting a good example and showing fans how to be who they were too.

To cement her status as down-to-earth Jessie, she spent Christmas with family, taking a long-overdue break. "Every Christmas, me and my dad were like: 'Next year's your year, next year's your year,'" she recalled to Neon Limelight. "And this Christmas was like: 'Oh my God, no shit, it's actually your year!' The pressure is crazy now."

Things were about to step up another notch when Jessie was presented with the Sound of 2011 Award and lauded as Britain's Next Big Thing. Every year, 160 music critics and taste-makers from across the UK were asked to nominate their favourite up-and-coming artist – someone they predicted would break through to full-scale fame that year. "If the idea of an Essex version of Katy Perry and Lady Gaga makes you shudder," *The Guardian* warned, "you'd better pack your bags now." However, it now seemed that being an Essex girl was all part of Jessie's appeal.

The county had suffered the reputation from hell over the years. Previously, its biggest claim to talent had been glamour model Jodie Marsh, who was more likely to adorn top-shelf magazines or be dubbed "Human Viagra" by randy tabloid journalists than show off any real accomplishments. At one point, her breasts were on show so often that they had become more recognisable than her face. Yet, for better or for worse, she was Essex's most famous ambassador.

Reality TV stars Jade Goody and Chantelle Houghton did little to counter the stereotype that had been afflicting Essex women ever since. However the tables turned when the county became known as the place to be if you were in the music business. *X Factor* finalists Stacey Solomon from Dagenham, Matt Cardle from Colchester – who won the 2010 show – and 2 Shoes from Southend had all proved that Essex had talent. It was coming back into fashion and working resolutely to earn itself a place on the map.

Soon, TV producers even turned its reputation for being ridiculed on its head by making it into a lucrative money-spinner, releasing a series called *The Only Way Is Essex*. Every week, more than 1.5 million viewers tuned in to catch a glimpse of these curious creatures they called Essex girls with their spray tans, buxom fake breasts and comical accents. The phrase "Shaaaat up!" – once derided as the epitome of common – was becoming the UK's new buzz phrase, and T-shirts with the slogan emblazoned across them were selling like hot cakes. The show, based around a nightclub in Brentwood called the Sugar Hut, depicted the reality stars flashing the cash – and made the county's new reputation all about spending power. Essex might have been just as cheap, trashy and irresistibly nasty as ever before – particularly after a few pints and a kebab following a night out at the Sugar Hut – but it was now becoming ever more expensive to look cheap. As *The Only Way Is Essex* star Amy Childs claimed: "We used to be known for white stilettos, but now it's [designer] Louboutin shoes."

The image of Essex had undergone a huge transformation – gone were the old tracksuits and hoop earrings, only to be replaced with Gucci handbags and designer shoes. For would-be fashionistas, penny pinching was no longer an option. Just like Coleen Rooney and Cheryl

Cole, so-called chavs and tramps were now fronting TV shows, gracing the front pages of high-fashion style magazines (Amy Childs had even ended up in *Vogue*) and emblazoned across gossip columns for dating some of the world's wealthiest footballers.

Coming from Essex was now something to be proud of – internet forums were flooded with messages from girls pleading for tips on how to perfect the "Essex girl image", while there were record increases on property searches in the region and one national dating website saw a 30 per cent rise in requests for women from Essex – all seemingly due to the show.

The image of Essex was changing fast – now that originating from there had the country's attention, perhaps her association with it was Jessie's chance to make an inroad with the public. Yet what did she herself think of the show? Exaggerating her accent, she told a venue in Sydney, Australia: "Shut up, oh my God, babe! You've totally gone over the top with that tan! I can smell the fumes from here, babes! That is what they talk like!"

The irony wasn't lost, even on an audience from the other side of the world – DVDs of the show had ended up on general release across the country. Jessie had even claimed that her name had been used on posters publicising promotional events for the show and claiming that she would be the host. It was news to Jessie, though. "I wasn't there!" she exclaimed. "It's nice that they appreciate that I'm from Essex and falsely using my name on posters!"

She added: "When it started taking off, everybody asked me if I watched it and I did. I watched it and I was so embarrassed. You know how it is with these programmes, they're so stereotypical of what exists – but sadly they *do* exist."

In spite of her embarrassment, the location she was born in had now become a boast rather than a shameful secret. *The Sun* reported: "Did you hear the one about the Essex girl who the nation ridiculed? Well, now she's the one having the last laugh. The once mocked females have risen above the hurtful jokes to become the It girls of the moment. Their tacky eighties reputation as dumb brassy blondes clad in stone-washed denim and tottering around in white stilettos is long gone. The modern Essex girl sports designer gear from head to toe, lives a VIP lifestyle and would not look out of place on the arm of a super-rich footballer."

Yet anyone expecting Jessie to fit the stereotype was in for a huge surprise. Fans of *The Only Way Is Essex* might have welcomed her origins with interest, but she was an unconventional Essex girl and – with her jet-black bob and gothic make-up – wouldn't have looked more out of a place in a Brentwood hotspot. While her accent was spot-on, the archetypal Essex girls could spend £600 a time on hair extensions, but for Jessie it wasn't about the price tag.

Not only that, but according to Amy Childs, "The most important thing in life is to look glamorous", while Jessie disapproved of society's obsession with perfection. "I'm not worried about making mistakes," she revealed to *This Is Essex.* "I'm sick of this idea that because I've been signed to a record label, I've got no cellulite, have perfect skin and a great arse. I'm a human being, my teeth aren't white and I get diarrhoea at the most awkward times, like everyone else. No one's perfect."

Her down-to-earth aspirations, which placed talent above a beautiful image, couldn't have been more different from Amy Childs' beliefs when she'd boasted: "We like our surgery, hair extensions, big eyelashes – we're very glitzy." Jessie, on the other hand, liked a bit of glamour as much as anyone, but she didn't make it her whole life – and she wasn't afraid to strip down to a bare face. Her lack of vanity came in stark contrast to the trend in her county for full-face perfection.

She wasn't the only one not to warm to the TV show. Mandie Holgate, the founder of the Essex Business Women's Network, raged: "The women portrayed in this programme seem to believe that taking their clothes off is the best way to make money and become famous. So much work has gone into changing the image of the Essex girl and this programme is taking us back years. The greatest damage is to the younger generation who don't have a strong sense of self. It sends them completely the wrong message."

At a time when some were frowning upon the new-found legacy of shows like *The Only Way Is Essex* and everything they promoted, branding them a culturally transmitted disease, could Jessie be carving out a niche for herself as the antithesis of a stereotypical bird-brained, image-obsessed Essex girl?

Her status as resident Essex woman was getting Jessie attention for all kinds of reasons, but soon she found herself accused of being the opposite – a spoiled rich kid. Many believed that she was pretending to be "street" to fit in with trends, disguising a secret background of wealth and privilege in the process. As she'd been to stage school, some felt that she couldn't cut it as an authentic urban artist – and they weren't afraid to say so.

One Digital Spy forum member blasted: "Jessie, we all know you studied musical theatre at the BRIT School, so pack it in with the 'I'm urban' shite. She's about as real as Shaun Ryder's teeth. It's kind of like Lily Allen, who tried hard to be 'chav' when we all know she is the daughter of a famous RICH comedian/actor and she apparently attended some of London's most exclusive boarding schools. Same with Jessie J posing as street when she went to stage school… it comes across as so fake and off-putting."

Another anonymous blogger added to the debate by criticising her "wannabe black routine". "I can't stand 'do it like a brother, do it like a man'dem' – what the fuck?" the blogger wrote. "Then you hear her in an interview and she sounds like Princess Diana."

In fact, Jessie's urban edge had been a result of growing up in a multicultural area, counting Jamaican and West African classmates as some of her closest friends. That also accounted for her wide vocabulary of ethnic slang words, "man'dem" included.

As for the Princess Diana comparisons, glossy high-society magazines had once written: "Is Princess Diana Essex?" after printing pictures of her dressed in white jeans – but that was the only similarity between Jessie with her regional twang and the royal with her clipped Sloaney-style accent.

YRB magazine supported Jessie too, arguing that she was far from a privileged princess. "When you hear an echo of Lily Allen's street slang in her lyrics, you remember this one's the real deal, brought up in the inglorious backwaters of Essex and learning her street-smarts on the hop," the magazine commented.

However, Jessie couldn't shake off her stage-school reputation, finding herself dismissed as just another cash-rich but talent-poor child of privilege. Adele had fuelled the rumours that the BRIT School was for the wealthy when she told the press that, unlike conventional schools, it had saved her from teenage pregnancy. "I hate to think where I'd have ended up if I hadn't gone to the BRIT School," she had told the *News Of The World*. "It's quite inspiring to be around 700 kids who want to be something – rather than 700 kids who just wanna get pregnant so they can get their own flat."

Many artists who were struggling to make it resented stage-school graduates, feeling they were offered an automatic springboard to success without needing to pay their dues. Some – little knowing that Jessie had once struggled herself – were angry that the school had produced one chart-topping famous singer after another, leaving others out in the cold. "I'm not saying that Amy Winehouse, Adele or Jessie J aren't talented but does anyone else think that young musicians/bands with just as much, and possibly even more, talent, who don't live in London are failing to be recognised because it's easy for the industry to rely on the BRIT School?" asked the website UKMix.

Frustratingly for Jessie, *Artrocker* was even less complimentary, claiming that she was just one in a long line of manufactured pop stars, like fellow BRIT graduates Kate Nash, Leona Lewis, Katie Melua, Luke Pritchard of The Kooks, The Noisettes and of course Amy Winehouse and Adele. "If Jessie J is the sound of 2011, should the rest of new music give up now?" it questioned. "The BBC's yearly predictive polling of 'taste-makers' increasingly states the bleeding obvious: naming an already hyped, industry-sponsored, stage school whelped Lady Gaga-lite singer as the most likely success story of the coming year is no huge stretch of their collective imaginations… it's worth highlighting the sad, incestuous nature of Jessie J's inexorable rise: as a BRIT School attendee, she has had the concerted weight of a desperate industry behind her from the start. If a public service broadcaster puts their weight behind her too, how do bands that are struggling to do it all alone feel?"

However, the BRIT School had been free of charge and, far from being an elitist institution, was open to anyone who could demonstrate that they had the talent. Was studying there really that unattainable if would-be entrants truly had the sound of the year themselves?

Leona Lewis hit back at the allegations of elitism too, countering: "My parents couldn't afford for me to go to [a fee-paying stage school] so [BRIT] is somewhere that's willing to give a chance to people that really want to do the performing arts and media," she told the BBC.

Meanwhile blogger Vic Word stepped in to defend Jessie from those she believed were merely venting their sour grapes that they hadn't been born talented. "No doubt going to the BRIT School has its advantages," she conceded. "But she only got in in the first place because of her talent and tenacity. Jessie J is going to be the first UK female to become a bona fide superstar in goodness knows how long. Why don't we save our complaints for when someone who isn't very good gets critical acclaim and try not to complain that the biggest British talent in years just won an award? Yes, there are struggling bands out there. But unless they're the next Coldplay, they really won't be a patch on Jessie."

Chapter 9

The Voice Money Couldn't Buy

"I was too loud – now I'm the sound of 2011!"

Jessie J

Jessie found herself public enemy number one yet again just days after being declared the sound of 2011. Industry accolades didn't always go hand in hand with happiness, as she was beginning to find out. Her former friend Amplify Dot, also known as MC A. Dot, had taken to the radio waves to deliver a snub in a rap. "I've seen friends turn into foes and I'll show you Exhibit A," A. Dot spat. "You know her as Jessie J, but I knew her back in the day – I won't say too much, but I poured my heart out all over the ray."

The shout-out came soon after a track the pair had performed on, 'Sweetest Thing', was leaked on to the internet. Perhaps A. Dot objected to the leak and blamed Jessie. Soon afterwards, A. Dot spoke to *RWD* to elaborate: "Our relationship isn't as harmonious as it used to be... it's a bit of a sticky one. It's weird how best friends can turn into foes. It's scary really, once you're put in this industry, how quickly things can change."

She added: "I'm hearing that it may be resolved by spring," adding weight to the theory that their dispute was a legal issue related to the track the two had written together.

However, perhaps that wasn't all that stood between them. Could A. Dot have been an ex-lover who found herself discarded when Jessie's career took off and left her unable to commit? A. Dot certainly looked like Jessie's type – she was the spitting image of her lover, Kira, so was it likely that the two had dated at some time in the past? Those in Jessie's inner circle had certainly heard that rumour, but they remained tight-lipped about the truth.

Or was it simply a case of jealousy on A. Dot's part? Jessie was topping charts, winning awards and was already tipped to be the next big thing, while her own career lagged behind. Jessie was telling the world that the roller-coaster ride she was on hadn't even started yet. It was clear that, far from being contented with a number one single, she had world domination in mind. What was more, at the tender age of 22, with her whole career stretching ahead of her, it looked as though she might just achieve it.

That might have been difficult news for A. Dot to swallow. When she'd first met Jessie, she'd been the more notorious one, receiving a promise from hip-hop legend Missy Elliott that she'd be "something big!" Yet while she struggled to get the acclaim in the industry she'd expected after those glowing references, it was now Jessie's name on everyone's lips – the tables had turned. Had A. Dot created the controversy to draw attention to her own music, or had it simply been a private dispute or matter of jealousy between them?

In any case, A. Dot's casual comment, "It's weird how best friends can turn into foes… once you're put in this industry", might have stuck in Jessie's throat. Whoever was to blame, fame had continued to have a drastic effect on her personal life. Not only did she find herself explaining to Twitter followers that she couldn't possibly respond to 4,000 Twitter messages a day, but she started needing to fight off admirers on a regular basis.

Everyone wanted a piece of her – and some wouldn't take no for an answer. "I've had someone lock themselves in the toilet next to me and then not let me leave the toilet," a terrified Jessie confided to gossip website 4TNZ. "It was quite scary because obviously there's that fine line between someone wanting to tell you that they love your music and then actually grabbing your arm so hard it really hurts. You're a bit like: 'It's okay, calm down!'"

The paparazzi were equally rabid in their desire to get her attention. "They shout out really horrible things to get a reaction and you just have to laugh and ignore them," she continued. "They're like, 'You smell!' and you're like: 'Okay, thank you!'"

Worst of all were the photographers in disguise – makeshift ones who wanted a picture to show their friends or sell on to the newspapers. One air stewardess even took a picture of Jessie while she slept on a flight. Miley Cyrus had found photos of her trading on the media market for $250,000 and more – and it seemed like Jessie might soon fall prey to the same fate.

A friend told the *Daily Star*: "Jessie doesn't know how she's going to cope with all the new attention she's getting. A few months ago, no one knew who she was and now she can't go out without someone shouting at her or wanting a picture."

If she ever refused, occasionally fans treated her with downright hostility. On one trip to the USA, Jessie tweeted: "Just left the TV studio and we R running late for the airport (not my fault). I couldn't stop 4 fans (wasn't allowed). Argh! Really breaks my heart. One ran to the lights and said 'Fuck you Jessie, fuck off back to the UK, you bitch' right next to the car, so now I'm tearful."

Paradoxically, while thousands of strangers now wanted a piece of Jessie – with some becoming hysterical – some of her closest friends couldn't handle the change and were going cold on her. One friend didn't want her to attend her birthday party because she worried all the attention would be on Jessie and her presence would overshadow her special day. There wasn't much she could do to control people's reactions and she began to resign herself to the changes. "You almost have to give people a little booklet," she told MSN sadly, "and say, 'This is how you now have to be my friend!'"

While rivalry and tension put her existing friendships to the test, she found that in any case, fame left her with little time to nurture her connections. When asked who she loved and if she was in a relationship she'd simply respond "I love me" and "I don't have time for relationships any more".

Allegedly, some people in Jessie's life were piling the pressure on her to keep her relationship with Kira – now rumoured to be an open one while the pair remained best friends – a secret. Not only did some feel she should protect Kira from the spotlight, but there were others who maintained that dating a woman – or dating anyone at all for that matter – could damage Jessie's career. In the eyes of the public, she had to maintain the pretence of being young, free and single. She was certainly young, but wasn't exactly single and, if reports were to be believed, had very little freedom. That was the price of fame.

"People didn't ask her not to be gay but they simply asked her if she would be comfortable in going along with something that meant she wouldn't immediately be tagged as 'that British lesbian singer'," a friend revealed. "She played the 'I don't label myself' card… and it caused tension between her and Kira."

Desperate to make an even bigger impact on British music than she had done thus far, Jessie felt torn in several conflicting directions. Only time made the pressure of being a Top 10 artist easier. "There are things that I probably thought were crazy, but it's just become normal to me now," she sighed to 4TNZ in resignation.

The public's obsession with her sexuality would come back to haunt her yet again in the months to come – but for now Jessie's attention was focused on her next big UK single, 'Price Tag'. The song's release was prefaced by a taster at a show at London's Scala club on January 18, where the British rapper Devlin replaced B.o.B. on his verse. It was talked up as the hottest show in town, with the *Evening Standard* speaking of "a singing voice so powerful it could play havoc with the earth's gravitational pull".

Twelve days later, in a bid to combat piracy, the song hit both the digital download shops and the radio waves on the same day. It was everywhere and, what was more, the message was strikingly different from anything else that graced the charts at the time. "It's about how too many people think that the world runs on money – but it doesn't," Jessie had argued. "It doesn't have to be about how many cars you've got, or how many necklaces you have. It's about the values and morals you have as a person."

'Price Tag' was her answer to rappers' chat about Lamborghinis, Ferraris, heavy gold chains and *Playboy* centrefolds. Kanye West was the king of conspicuous consumption, despite claiming he only flashed the cash in his rhymes because "wags wanna hear it".

Yet it wasn't just the rap world that craved material things – Jessie was taking on the R&B camp too. In fact, even down-to-earth Beyoncé wasn't immune from the financial bragathon. In 'Upgrade You', after partner Jay-Z scoffs at her desire to upgrade him, asking how he could ever climb higher than number one – a reference to his chart position – she responds by name-checking designer cufflinks, credit cards without limits and six-star "pimp suites". The message was clear – money meant status and, no matter how much he had, he could always do with some more.

Chatting about the cash even comes up in tender ballads like 'Flaws And All' where she lists being a "pauper" compared to some big spenders as one of her biggest weaknesses. Even as an enormously wealthy multimillionaire with every asset the average person could dream of, Beyoncé still had her mind on her money.

It was an increasingly competitive world, with singers finding themselves under unrelenting pressure to be the best – but their worth wasn't always defined by their tunes. Celebrity magazines would devote double-page spreads to a singer's new mansion, or report admiringly on the diamond-encrusted handbag that she might have bought for her designer dog. For the men, meanwhile, it was about how many bottles of Cristal champagne they could down in the club, or how many lap dancers were surrounding them.

Jessie was on a mission to change that. She felt that, in their eagerness to prove their supremacy, singers sometimes let the music get left behind. "I'm bored of hearing so many of these new up-and-coming rappers spit about how sick they are and they're gonna fuck up the game," she tweeted.

The rapper stereotype was about to be challenged even further when B.o.B. appeared in person to perform on the 'Price Tag' video. It was loaded with irony. She declared war on the macho-man type that she'd parodied on 'Do It Like A Dude' when a scene of her grabbing her crotch from that promo appeared on 'Price Tag' as she sang pointedly about "video hoes".

In one scene, viewers see Jessie cramming herself into a tiny doll's house. Whether a blow-up sex doll or a child's plaything, the imagery of a doll represented an object without a will of its own that could be manipulated by the person using it. It might have looked pretty and perfect on the outside, but underneath it had no mind of its own.

The video also depicts puppets which need their strings pulled to be able to perform. Without an outside force to control their movements, they are benign and useless. A wind-up ballerina inside a music box completes the metaphor.

The video seemed to parody pop stars who were moulded into a sound or image until they were on trend and financially marketable even if it meant not being themselves. Jessie rebelled against that with the message: "Be who you are." Her parody seemed to poke fun at people who would sell anything – from their bodies to their souls and true identities – to be rich and famous. It exposed those who would live their lives in obedient servitude to powerful taste-makers within the industry in order to make it big. Such people had been enslaved by their desire to portray a fantasy image of both financial wealth – and, in the case of the doll metaphor – physical perfection. Jessie even mocks the girls who soldier on in their attempts to dance wearing ankle-wrenchingly high stilettos, thrusting a bright pink heel at the camera as she sings about it.

However, an uplifting message seems to come in the form of a torn teddy bear with an eye missing. The bear might have seen better days and it might not have been brand new or perfect, but a child could cuddle and be comforted by it nonetheless – it could still be someone's beloved toy. The teddy bear is Jessie's defiant challenge to the need for perfection, or the need to compete for purchase power to buy the newest and glossiest things. As she dances around a money tree with dollar notes sprouting from its branches, she makes the message clear – life might be about love, happiness and music, but it's not about the price tag, as the most important things in life are free.

However, spoof website Vigilant Citizen thought otherwise. According to them, Jessie's "OK" gesture – encircling a thumb and forefinger around her eye – was a sign that she was a devil worshipper and a member of the Illuminati. "I don't even know what the hell it is," Jessie spluttered to Q magazine. "[But] people have written seven-page essays on how I worship the Devil!"

Not only that, but the website insisted she was a victim of "mind control". "A mutilated teddy bear alludes to a corrupted childhood," it read. "Teddy bears with no limbs have a specific meaning referring to the helplessness of mind control victims versus their handlers. The teddy bear the child is given by her daddy is to remind her how helpless she is to prevent him from raping her." The essay continued that even something as innocuous as her leopard-print leggings – which video director Emil Nava explained as bringing a "fashion edge" to the video – is a "code for Sex Kitten Programming".

Ludicrously, the claims fuelled a hate campaign against Jessie and she started to receive a flurry of letters claiming that 'Do It Like A Dude' played backwards was a message from Satan. Others wrote that they were praying – to the Devil, no doubt – for her to get HIV and throat cancer both at the same time, so that they would never hear her voice again.

However, her father hadn't told her that humour was the best therapy for nothing – and she laughed off the cruel comments. She tweeted: "Jeez, people, I'm doing the 'OK' sign over my eye. No 666 around here… No, thank you!" She later returned to add: "NO, I DO NOT BELIEVE IN THE ILLUMINATI, NOR AM I INVOLVED IN IT. FACT! PUT THAT IN THE PAPER!"

However, Jessie faced more serious criticism from the newspapers, some of which rejected her sentiments about money. *The Observer* claimed: "Jessie… asserts that music, and indeed life, may not all be about the 'chi-ching' and the 'bli-bling'. Hard to fathom, but this is news to some people." It added: "It is, of course, quite disingenuous to sing 'We don't need your money, money, money' when that is precisely what you need to sustain a career that you have worked for since childhood."

Despite her best efforts, Jessie was still being typecast as a spoiled stage-school brat on account of her background in musical theatre. Critics insisted that her street guise and socialist values didn't erase the background of privilege that they imagined she had risen from.

However, had Jessie brought on some of the criticism herself? Just two weeks before the song's release, she had told *The Mirror*: "I want this voice to buy me a house, a car…" Meanwhile, according to *The Times*, she felt she was "living the dream… finally earning some money and being able to buy myself a nice handbag".

Some might say her comments invited criticism, as they seemed to be in stark contrast to the message the song delivered. If life wasn't really about the money, why was she already planning all the things her 'Price Tag' pay cheque could buy? Was it a mere coincidence that a track that said so was doubtless making her a millionaire? And was she is danger of becoming one of the very people her song spoke out against? Even BRIT School friend Kerry Louise Barnaby took a swipe at her, commenting: "If it's not all about the money, give the song away for free!"

However, while Jessie might have been seduced by a metallic Louis Vuitton must-have handbag as much as the next fashionista, she might have argued in her defence that a penchant for designer goodies didn't make her a slave to money.

Instead it seemed she was rebelling against those who filled their entire lives with financial excess and superficiality at the expense of their songs – those who put everything money could buy ahead of their craft and their God-given talents. After all, a voice like hers wasn't up for sale in the shops – was it so wrong to want to be recognised for it?

Yet some of the critics continued to tear her to pieces, feeling that for someone whose selling point was that she didn't value money, she was attaching a lot of prominence to it. What was more, some of her statements seemed to contradict each other. She'd told *Sugarscape*: "I've always said style should not be a brand" but she'd been wearing D&G at award ceremonies, then telling the world she was thrilled to be dressed in Vivienne Westwood for the first time at her Scala show. She was soaking up all the perks of a celebrity lifestyle, with free designer threads and living life large all part of the territory.

She'd told *Time Out*: "I'm loving it, now I get to wear Vivienne Westwood clothes for a day and then give them back!" but, contrastingly, she'd told *I Like Music*: "I don't want to be a throwaway – like, 'I'm going to a party and I get free clothes!' and all that crap. I'm about the music." Was this a tale of two Jessies – a modest-living, music-loving one and her materialistic evil twin?

Politics aside, it was definitely about the music for her fans when 'Price Tag' hit the charts. It sailed straight to the top, selling 84,000 copies in its very first week. "It feels like the fun is back in the charts, you don't know what's going to happen now," Jessie smiled to *The Big Issue*. "It initially went in at number 247 and two days later, it was number one."

Not only that, but Jessie also declared her revenge on Lady Gaga by preventing her single, 'Born This Way', from debuting at number one. She'd told earlier of how Gaga had "made normal artists and music boring" due to her headline-grabbing outlandish dress sense but, several weeks after its release, Jessie was still ahead of her pop rival in the rankings, while Gaga stayed on the "edge of glory". Maybe "normal" artists weren't so boring after all.

Her school friend Adele was a serious competitor for chart status, though. After two weeks of holding the number one position, Jessie was knocked off the top spot by her single 'Someone Like You'. This news had led to some crude jokes from the public, with fans who knew of her sexuality joking: "Adele knocked her off", only for others to reply: "That's one sex tape I shall be avoiding!"

However, Jessie had the last laugh as her CDs sailed off the shelves. What's more, it wasn't just a success on home turf. The song was concurrently released in the USA as the lead single and peaked at number 23 on the *Billboard* chart – quite a feat for someone who'd never played a public concert there and who, outside of showbiz circles, was almost totally unknown. She even debuted at number one in New Zealand, another uncharted territory for Jessie.

Yet the plans for world domination were just beginning, as Jessie had finally finished recording the album. "It has taken a long time," she confessed to *I Like Music*. "I had to fight for my songs, for 'Stand Up', 'Casualty Of Love', 'Big White Room' and 'Mamma Knows Best' – there were times when [the label] weren't even sure if they liked 'Who You Are'!"

The tussles hadn't just been about her own material, either. Her mentors had longed for her to take influence from other hits like Katy Perry's 'I Kissed A Girl' – a sound Jessie had never been fond of. Not only that, but while Katy openly admitted the track was a marketing ploy, Jessie had wanted to be honest about who she was – both sound-wise and on a personal level.

In a world where glamour, sex and scandal sold, was Jessie finding it hard to be true to herself in the industry? She'd prided herself on relating to her fans by being a "normal girl", not an unreachable superstar – someone who strived to bring "goodness" to the world and to use music as therapy. An admirable aspiration – but did normal sell? Jessie was the sound of 2011, but – without outrageous antics – would she stand the test of time and be the talk of 2011, and 2012, too?

It was hard for her when the other girls in the music world were determined to keep it crazy. Gaga's outrageous costumes made headlines around the world – so much so that, when she was snapped in normal dress and heels – glamorous by most people's standards but far from her usual eccentric style – she attracted more attention than the time she wore a dress made from slabs of meat. Her stage clothes had become expected everyday wear.

Meanwhile Cheryl Cole was just as much a sex symbol and a fashion icon to her followers she was a singer – some might say more so – and Jessie admitted to feeling insecure that she "couldn't compete" with her beauty. The Jessie of 2011 was neither a glamour girl with a philandering footballer on her arm nor a preacher's daughter dressing up as a nun in a latex fetish outfit. She wasn't collecting an award with raw meat wrapped around her naked body and she wasn't suspending herself from the ceiling before jumping through a trapeze. There was no shock value.

Jessie was pretty, but not ostentatiously beautiful. She was edgy, but not over the top. She was controversial but she refused to be offensive – declining even to sing the word "motherfucker" live on stage. Where did she fit?

She addressed the issue when she vented to *The Mirror*: "Gaga is incredible, but she's set the bar so high for everyone else. She's made normal artists and music 'boring' which really bothers me." She added: "It pisses me off when people say Leona [Lewis] is boring. No, she's not. Personally, I don't do the style thing to be an artist that people can't relate to. I'm no fantasy artist."

Jessie was trying to keep it real – but at what cost? Was it proving to be a battle between commercial success and true identity? Did she struggle to choose between being famous and being herself? Finally, was she under pressure to be outrageous and different to keep up with so-called "fantasy artists" like Gaga, even though that wasn't where her heart was at?

It seemed the answer was yes when she told Clayton Perry: "I don't want to be here to come and go. I want to be here to stay and if that means I have to wear some crazy outfits and some crazy lip jewellery to stay in the game, I will do it because I want the music to shout louder than the outfit."

She was even keen to change her weight to boost her popularity, telling the *Daily Star*: "I need to eat more… Most people say they need to eat less [but] I need to stock up on carbs because a bum sells more records." She had lamented several times in the press already that, despite owning skyscraper legs, she had been "at the back of the queue for boobs and bum" when God was handing physical assets out.

Jessie's comment about a bigger bottom might have been an ironic one however, fuelled by her mischievous sense of humour. She'd let her loose tongue get her in trouble once before when she joked to a journalist that she wanted to write a song for Britney Spears about crotch-grabbing. Although Rihanna had previously told the world she wanted to spank Britney on screen and had been left unscathed, Jessie's jokey comment had been taken badly. She had found herself taking to Twitter to defend: "I'm learning that in interviews over the phone, my WORDS are very often TWISTED and when people DON'T get my humour, my JOKES are written as FACTS. LOL, oh well."

So perhaps Jessie hadn't been serious about boosting her bottom J-Lo style either. However, she did seem to be saying she felt obliged to play up her image for publicity to stay at the forefront of music lovers' minds. She'd admitted that Lady Gaga was making life difficult by being so controversial that other artists failed to compete and risked being written off as bores if they didn't plaster their bodies in raw meat or don a giant fake lobster on their head as a hat. Yet it was hard to compete with a woman who wore shoes that looked more like stilts.

Her plight echoed the fictional story told in Destiny's Child's 'Nasty Girl', where Beyoncé and co. complained that "trashy" girls in barely there outfits made it hard for more conservative girls with morals who still wanted to attract men. The video had parodied "sleazy" and classless women who dressed in miniskirts and tiny crop tops for something as simple as a trip to the supermarket.

The issue for Jessie wasn't one of sleaze, but – perhaps – of being eccentric enough to maintain her place in the headlines. First had come the spiked shoulder pads and the glittery lip spikes, then the slashed minidresses and Mickey Mouse ears, closely followed by a bright purple wig.

How much of this was shock tactics and how much was it simply Jessie expressing her own sense of style? After all, she'd said the lip jewellery was about staying in the game. Was she transforming herself into a visual prostitute just to stay in the music business – and didn't all of this contradict her message to be who you are?

Perhaps, but it sounded as if the true message was getting through and the music *was* shouting louder than the outfits, as she'd hoped. Why? One morning, Jessie had logged on to the internet to find that her song had saved a fan from suicide. "When you receive messages like, 'I was ready to take my own life last week and I decided not to when I heard "Who You Are"' – that, for me, should be on the front page of the papers," she told Clayton Perry. "That's the most humbling feeling you can ever have at 22 years old."

Not only that, but Jessie understood – the song had saved her life, too. Before penning it, she'd been so frustrated she was ready to give up music altogether. Yet after pouring out her frustration in the studio, the song had ended up the title track of her debut album, one that would be leading her to the top of the charts. Like Amy Winehouse, she had turned her pain into beautiful music – and she'd saved someone's life in the process.

She showed her commitment to being who she was yet again when she vowed to stay teetotal – and not be ashamed of it. It was the biggest day of her career thus far on February 15 when she arrived at the BRIT Awards in London to receive the Critics' Choice Award – but if the paparazzi were hoping to sneak a shot of her playing up to her Essex girl stereotype and vomiting blood backstage that night from overindulgence, they would be in for a huge disappointment. Jessie was sticking to her guns, no matter how much she might be ridiculed for it. "I think it's a blessing in disguise that I can't abuse my body the way some people do," she told the BBC in defiance. "I remember when I won, people were like: 'You don't drink, so how are you going to celebrate?' and I think it's really sad that people associate getting drunk with having fun. That's not how I roll. I think it's really important for people to know that that's not the only way to have fun."

Success was the biggest adrenalin rush of all that night. The Critics' Choice Award was a chance for the media to vote for their favourite British newcomer – the one they predicted would be the name on everyone's lips that year. Many of the acts were virtually unknown to the British public at the time that they were nominated, so it was an opportunity to showcase her talents to an audience who were equally keen to be in on the next big thing. Over a hundred newspaper, magazine and website editors, along with TV and radio producers, had spoken – and Jessie's name had come out on top.

The award had been a woman's world with no dudes in sight. The previous three years had seen Ellie Goulding, Florence & the Machine and Adele claim the prize and, after beating James Blake and The Vaccines to the top, Jessie was ensuring 2011 would be no exception. "For the last few years, the girls who have won it have set the bar for UK female artists," she told the *Daily Record*. "To be among those people is like a dream come true. I feel like I am going to cry."

On learning of her success, she told one journalist: "I said I would go speechless if I'd heard I'd won a BRIT, but we have to keep talking!"

Jessie had to keep up the conversation with her thrilled friends too, who couldn't wait to be her dates for the ceremony. "[They] were all like: 'Where are we going to to be sitting?' and, 'Will we be able to talk to you?'" Jessie joked to *Gigwise*. "I was like, 'Calm down and chill out!'"

Yet when the big moment finally arrived, Jessie was anything but calm and collected. As she was handed her award by 2010 winner Ellie Goulding and super-producer Mark Ronson, she was reduced to tears.

"There aren't many times in my life when I'm speechless!" she gulped. "[This is] for anyone who's been with me on my journey... thank you for making my dreams come true."

She later told the *Evening Standard* that she was "overwhelmed", adding: "I've been doing this for six years [but] now I'm doing it in front of the world rather than in my bedroom and posting it on YouTube. So many people are saying that music is dead. That's why I'm here. I want to be an icon for the UK. On the world stage I'm an ambassador for the UK and I'm so proud to be wearing our flag."

Jessie was voting for England all the way, but a little mischief had been on her mind when she joked prior to the ceremony: "I was thinking of putting on an American accent and then be like, 'Sorry about that, come on Essex!'" She'd also joked that she'd be coming to the event in her pyjamas to prove she was still down to earth, but the reality was much more glamorous. "We went to the Universal after-party and I was the only one wearing colour," she told Gigwise. "I was in these amazing Versace pants and everyone else was in black suits, I looked like a right one!"

Yet whether in brightly coloured Versace or a pair of tatty PJs, Britain had voted – and she was officially a star.

Chapter 10

A Rhythm For Life

"Can you imagine me with alcohol? I'm irritating enough without it all!"
Jessie J

*T*he Guardian might have dismissed her as "an Essex version of Katy Perry and Lady Gaga" but Jessie set out to prove she was much, much more than that – and she hoped the album would silence her critics all by itself.

She didn't have to wait long before her ultimate defence weapon arrived. *Who You Are* was Jessie's baby – the one she'd spent six years perfecting – and, after an extraordinarily long pregnancy and a few near miscarriages, it was finally ready. Due to overwhelming public demand, the release date was pushed forward by a month, hitting the UK's shops on February 28.

But the backlash was about to begin. To some, every song was controversial. Offended macho men were frothing at the mouth over 'Do It Like A Dude', while in 'Rainbow', at a time when immigration tensions over jobs were at an all-time high, Jessie cheerily invited the world, regardless of nationality or creed, to share their pot of gold.

What was more, a common complaint was that, contrary to the album's title, whoever she was on CD, it wasn't herself. *The Guardian* claimed:

Who You Are doesn't tell us a lot about who she is: she's confident, she's fortunate, she's real, she believes in herself. But these noble qualities are what everybody raised to the purple of celebrity has in common."

Metro added: "It's not entirely clear what kind of artist Jessie J wants to be on *Who You Are* or whether her heart lies in R&B pop", and finally the *NME* concurred: "No matter how much Jessie J sings about being herself, we don't really ever get a sense of who, or what, that is."

The widespread criticism seemed to have come about because Jessie refused to tie herself down to one genre of music. Some might say she was diverse and well-rounded, but other reviewers were implying a full-on identity crisis. With the jazzy burlesque sound of 'Mamma Knows Best', the reggae-themed 'Stand Up', the Rihanna-style pop swagger of 'Do It Like A Dude' and the tender, confessional big-ballad vibe of 'Big White Room', no two songs were the same – she was delivering a variety pack.

Some said this meant the public didn't get a sense of who she was – if she even knew herself – but Jessie had an answer for her detractors, and she was prepared to defend her decisions to the death. "I don't ever want to put my music in a hole, in a pigeon box hole, where people feel like if I step out of it, it's, 'Jessie J lost her love for what she does' or, 'Jessie J takes a risk with something new!'" she explained to Global Grind. "I think you should get people used to the fact that I don't always sound the same, that my consistency is in my voice and my personality."

In fact, the album was as much a roller-coaster of variety as Jessie's life had been over the years trying to find fame. "It wasn't just 'Do It Like A Dude' and 'Price Tag', it's not like 14 versions of that song," she explained to *I Like Music*. "Releasing 'Do It Like A Dude' and then 'Price Tag', people already know the album is not going to be same, same, same, same. There are ballads, reggae, pop, there's rap a little bit. It represents how I saw life going from a 17-year-old to a young adult."

Her last words on the matter were to *PrideSource*, defiantly countering anyone who dared to say she wasn't singing in a way that reflected who she was. "I don't feel like I have to say I'm pop or I'm rock or I'm hip hop," she claimed. "I make music and if people like it, they like it. I think it gets people frustrated because they need to pigeonhole me but I won't allow them to, because I just think it's about being who you are."

Jessie's fans were equally ferocious in defending the album's diversity. One blogger raged: "You do her a disservice by saying it's a record of two halves – what's wrong with that? She can do anything and that is an asset, not a drawback. Please don't say she can be a British Katy Perry or P!nk, why the eff would she wanna be them? She's just Jessie J!"

In spite of the protests, the pigeonholing continued when the BBC claimed: "Hearing a BRIT School girl from London's suburbs deliver lines derived from Caribbean slang is uncomfortable." However, hailing from a multicultural background, Jessie might simply reply with the lyrics of 'Rainbow'.

Yet even that song stirred fresh controversy among the critics when they questioned, not for the first time, how a supposedly wealthy "brat" who'd wanted for nothing all her life and had the spare cash to indulge in ballet lessons every week could ever hope to understand the plight of a struggling single mother in the ghetto. *The Independent*, for example, complained: "Jessie's taste for feel-good cliché gets the better of her. Comparing the spend-thrift life of a privileged rich kid with the plight of the inner-city poor, she somehow reaches the demonstrably nonsensical conclusion that 'we're all alike'."

To add to the controversy, the album coincided with newspaper reports that 289,000 jobs had gone to foreigners while one in five young British-born people remained on benefits. However, Jessie's song had risen above the politics with an uplifting anthem against bigotry and racism – one of the type that might have had Nick Griffin of the BNP shaking his fist in fury.

Meanwhile, Jessie's passion for reggae was in the right hands; Island Records founder Chris Blackwell was not just half Jamaican himself, but he'd also been the man to introduce the world to Bob Marley.

At that time, only one other young white female artist was experimenting with the genre, combining reggae beats with pure and simple pop, and that was Lily Allen. It had led to unfavourable comparisons between them, with *Pitchfork Media* claiming that Jessie "sounds like a severely dumbed down Lily Allen at best and at worst she seems like someone you would want to root against in a televised singing competition." However the same site had been equally damning about Amy Winehouse's debut album and she'd then exceeded all expectations with two multi-platinum-selling albums and a string of prestigious awards. More importantly, it wasn't the bloggers that Jessie had to impress, but the listeners.

Indeed, the critics might have snubbed it but the public loved it. When the day of reckoning came, the CD debuted at number one in the UK chart and went on to sell over 600,000 copies in the UK alone, making it one of the most popular albums of the year.

Plus the tidal wave of media negativity was tempered by a few glowing reviews. Virgin Media said that Jessie would be one of the "biggest and coolest UK female artists for decades" while *The Guardian* claimed: "This album brims with infectious Americanised songs, delivered with a confidence money can't buy."

The album even had a public shout-out from singer and former *X Factor* judge Dannii Minogue. She'd seen Jessie strutting her stuff on the BRIT Awards red carpet in a catsuit but, living thousands of miles across the world in Melbourne, she knew little about her music. That all changed when the radio campaign for 'Price Tag' took off in Australia. "I was driving to the airport to fly off to *Australia's Got Talent* auditions on the Gold Coast when I first heard the single on the radio and yes, by the time the chorus rolled around for the second time, it was, 'Woahhhh, I love that song!'" she blogged. "It had me singing along at the top of my lungs and getting some seriously raised eyebrows from my manager and all the drivers of the cars that had the misfortune of stopping next to me at the traffic lights."

It seemed as though Jessie's music was now wooing celebrities and stopping traffic – something she couldn't have imagined back in the days when she would make humble music videos in her bathroom and post them to a few friends on YouTube.

Dannii continued: "I see Jessie J as a bit of a British Rihanna and I can't wait to check out what she's going to rock out on the red carpet next. And, if the YouTube clip I watched of her singing an acoustic version of 'Price Tag' on *Later With Jools Holland* is anything to go by, she's a woman with a killer live vocal!"

It seemed to some as though Jessie had redeemed herself – and, what was more, the album soon peaked at number four in Australia. Apart from a few promotional appearances there, when she'd shared her frustrations with Aussies about "narrow-minded people" putting all Essex girls into a pigeonhole, she'd never played in the country, but that was soon set to change.

Jessie had also set her sights on the USA. She'd released 'Casualty Of Love' on iTunes there, a song specifically chosen to appeal to American tastes. Just as 'Do It Like A Dude' had been right on trend for the UK, with a mix of the urban and ethnic influences that were storming the British chart at that time, 'Casualty Of Love' had been hand-picked for American ears, with a soul vibe like Alicia Keys' 'If I Ain't Got You', which matched the typical sound of the airwaves stateside.

Meanwhile the campaign stepped up a notch when she was booked to appear on the national show *Saturday Night Live*, before her album had even hit the shops. Speaking of her March 12 performance, the *Los Angeles Times* exclaimed: "It made her one of the first to appear on the show without an album on shelves – a fact that still boggles the mind."

Jessie was as terrified as the critics might have expected, but she was determined that it was the right thing to do. "I want to sit there with the Katy Perrys and the Gagas and the Rihannas and feel comfortable," she insisted to *The Mirror*. "I don't want to be the chick who tried to make it and didn't. I'm not going to sleep until that happens."

Did Jessie have many sleepless nights in store, or would the public take to her? As frightening as it was, it was time to find out. "The producers were taking a risk," she told the *Los Angeles Times*. "It was the scariest, most nerve-racking thing in the world. Nobody had any idea who I was. I'd done no promos. It was purely, like, get out there and sing. I've always been someone who loved a challenge and I don't like things given to me easily."

Jessie had a very American attitude to success – she couldn't spend too much time on gushing modesty or on perfecting her airs and graces. She was a go-getter, she was there for the fame and she wasn't going to stop until she got it – exactly the attitude she needed to break a country like America. In a world of tough, outspoken, ultra-competitive, shamelessly arrogant self-believers, if Jessie performed well, the first question they were going to ask was why she hadn't launched herself sooner.

But now Jessie didn't just have her own self-belief to fall back on; one of the country's most influential taste-makers had her back. Jason Flom claimed of his decision to push her all the way stateside: "If you believe in your heart and soul that something is the real thing, then you have to be willing to stake your reputation on it."

What did America think? Blog site The Truth About Music was unimpressed, sneering: "When a quote in *Rolling Stone* reads 'The UK's answer to Lady Gaga', you had better bring it", before concluding: "Making Gaga comparisons can't possibly be worth the pressure... Jessie failed in her mission to be the UK's Lady Gaga. At this point, she'll be lucky to be the UK's answer to Miley Cyrus."

These were harsh words for Jessie, and not an ideal introduction. Yet in contrast, one anonymous A&R exec blogged: "Those eyes might look like they belong to Katy Perry, but trust that Jessie J is quite possibly the antithesis of Utah's Teenage Nightmare... She's not some faux punk-rock update on the saccharine sweet Katy Perry model."

That was good news for Jessie because, while she aspired to be just as much a household name as Katy – if not more so – she couldn't stand the comparisons. She had defended in the press: "It's sad because I've only ever tried to be me." Yet some understood, and the review concluded by calling 'Do It Like A Dude' a "hyper-visceral eargasm".

However, there was another crushing setback in store to throw her off the path of her American invasion when 'Being Britney', the song she'd written for Spears' album, *Femme Fatale*, didn't make the cut. She'd hoped to be as big as every last one of the country's icons and an association with Britney, who had once been described as "an all-American girl" and "the American dream personified", would have been perfect. Yet it had been another near-miss.

"I think it's a misunderstanding that just because I'm Jessie J, it doesn't mean that I get pumped up to the top three choice – it means that I write a song," Jessie explained to MTV. "If it doesn't go on [the album], it doesn't go on it. She probably had every major songwriter in the world write a song for her... I'm still taking baby steps."

Not to be defeated, Jessie fought back with "I'll just write a better song [next time]." Plus she could seek solace in the knowledge that she was a competent writer – more than many had been saying about Britney. As *Femme Fatale* hit the stores, she began to field criticism for not co-writing a single track on the album. The media were questioning whether she was truly a singer or just a performing puppet.

As the harsh glare of the media spotlight encircled Britney, one of her writers, Heather Bright, who'd co-penned the song 'Trouble For Me', stepped in to none too subtly set the record straight. "I would just like to address one thing," she blogged. "The media is talking trash about how Britney didn't write one of the songs on her album... HELLO! Wake up, everybody! NONE OF THESE ARTISTS WRITE THEIR OWN SONGS!!!!!!!"

She concluded that there were "a few exceptions", name-checking Lady Gaga and Chris Brown, before continuing: "Anyway, Britney could have come to me, like all these other A-list artists and said: 'Hey, you wanna be on my album? I'm gonna need writing credit for that song AND part of your publishing royalties even though I didn't write anything! And then I'm gonna go on tour, gross $150 million in ticket sales and not give you any of that, even though I'm performing your song! I could rattle off a laundry list of artists who I've had that conversation with!"

While scores of chart-topping performers were publicly humiliated by the allegations, Jessie could stand tall and take comfort in the fact that 'Big White Room', one of the tracks on her top-selling album, had been penned by nobody but herself. The blog website Music And Mayhem had passed her off as "just another hype" and sneered: "There's something about her that just screams manufactured" , but some of her repertoire had been written long before the taste-makers had come into her life.

Plus she wasn't merely a lyric writer, like some of the artists who bagged writing credits – she also wrote melodies, at the rate of four to five a week. "I like to write with melody and lyric at the same time," she told *I Like Music*. "For me, it's about delivery and emotion... the melody should team with the lyrics as much as the lyrics should team with the melody – and I'm still learning!" No matter what the haters might have told the world, it seemed that this was just the beginning of her journey.

The writing offers had started to come thick and fast from people who believed she wasn't just a singer but a competent composer as well. Christina Aguilera had been back in touch and 2010 *X Factor* winner Matt Cardle was also looking for new tracks. However one of the offers had come from a camp that made Jessie feel a little uncomfortable – singer and actor Will Smith's 10-year-old daughter Willow was looking for a rhyme. "I've been sent a beat from Willow's management, but what do you write about for her?" Jessie had asked. "She's so young. Perhaps 'I grabbed my lunchbox, I went to school...?' Haha! I can only write songs that have been shoes I've walked in."

Jessie was a hit with the celebrity crowd, but she was also in just as much demand with the public, and, as interest in the album grew, so did speculation about her sexuality.

She'd been open from the start. At one of her first-ever UK headline appearances, at the Camden Barfly on February 6, she had started freestyling into the mic, rapping: "Jessie J, is she gay or is she straight? Boy or a girl, it don't matter to me."

If that hadn't cleared up the rumours, three weeks later on February 26, she had played London's G-A-Y club and dedicated 'L.O.V.E.' to a girl. She'd described the show as a "super-fun gig – lots of confetti and wind and random explosions throughout the set". However, the most explosive element of all for an audience of excited lesbians came when Jessie chose to open up about her sexuality. "I had to talk about it, just because it's G-A-Y, you know, to see if there were any hotties in the crowd," she laughed to *PrideSource*.

It turned out that the gay community loved Jessie as much as she loved them – they'd found in her a new avatar for alternative sexuality. GaydarNation declared her "hot property" before delivering a put-down to one of her arch rivals. "Not to be confused with Katy Perry, whose own lesbian club dancefloor filler 'I Kissed A Girl' was ultimately created to titillate straight men," the website asserted. "Jessie J's 'Do It Like A Dude', on the other hand, celebrates masculine women at the same time as it turns the tables on the sexist music industry dominating the charts today."

While the gay community seemed to understand where she was at, the wider world did not. Week after week, magazines and websites would "exclusively reveal" that Jessie had dated girls, even though she'd never hidden it. One post on her Twitter account had read: "For all the people congratulating me on 'coming out' or confirming I'm bi, LOL, I have NEVER hidden my sexuality. The press just like to grasp anything and make it gossip... I love who I love. I will never label my sexuality. If it's a boy, it's a boy. If it's a girl, it's a girl." She later added: "I will never apologise for anything that makes me happy. No one should :) Whatever I do in life, SOMEONE somewhere will HATE it. Be it my music, my face, my clothes, my hair, my bum, LOL. It is what it is. Let the haters hate. Live for the moment."

She also let loose on the radio show *In Demand*, when she reiterated: "I've never denied it. Whoopie doo guys, yes, I've dated girls and I've dated boys – get over it. It's not a secret, but it's the only thing [people] can grab onto. They're like: 'She never drinks and she comes out of the party looking like she did when she went in, damn her!'"

That seemed to be the end of the matter. Yet, close to Jessie's inner circle, the rumours that she was secretly 100 per cent lesbian, but claiming not to label herself, could not be repressed. On the other side of the coin, outsiders were infuriated with her claims, believing she was playing up to a trend by embracing lesbian chic.

What could go wrong? After all, she'd have male fans panting, their trousers straining at the groin, some buying tickets to her shows purely to see the girl of their threesome fantasies up close and personal. Jessie would appeal to straight girls too, those who wanted to impress their boyfriends and seem daring, risqué and cool – as well as the ones who genuinely wanted to experiment. She'd stand out in the industry like Katy Perry and earn extra brownie points for a lifestyle that was slightly different. She'd attract a number of fans purely for the novelty value – and that was before her music had even entered the equation.

With that theory in mind, some of the public disputed that her sexuality was a scam, a publicity stunt, at the expense of people who were questioning their sexuality in real life. One Digital Spy forum member raged: "It annoys me because I have gay and bisexual friends who have genuinely been through hell coming to terms with their sexual identity and these people wear it like a bloody designer belt. I can maybe forgive teenage girls trying to look cool and thinking it increases their sexual desirability – but grown women in their twenties? No, no, no."

The blogger saw Jessie's sexuality as a fashion statement and a way to titillate and attract attention from men, not to mention boost her record sales. Was it an insult to people who had to live with their sexuality for life, while the fakers could use theirs like a label and peel it off when it no longer fitted society?

Another forum member felt people had been too quick to judge. After all, had they been a fly on the wall in Jessie's bedroom? And how else could they make their claims with such confidence? "I think some are mistakenly linking Jessie in with this new celebrity trend of saying they are bi to be cool," she argued. "With her, I really don't think this is the case. As anyone with access to Google and who cares enough will find, her most recent exes prior to being famous were women. She confirmed it in an interview to stop the press from running a story and outing her."

Jessie echoed all that the anonymous blogger had said, telling *PrideSource*: "I've never hidden it and I've been in this industry for six years. I've had partners with me all the time. I've introduced them to everybody – every producer, every songwriter... It's only since I've come into the limelight that it's been made this media thing. You can never prove it and people are going to think what they want to think, but I know the truth. I know I would never, ever [fake my sexuality to gain attention] because I wouldn't want my sexuality to define my music and I wouldn't want it to define me. It's only now that I talk about it because people feel the need to hear about it. And I'm honest about it. Why should I lie?"

To Jessie, it was "about the person, not the genitals", and she felt that it was society which sought to put people in categories. However, it was not the boys but the girls she was lusting after whenever she spoke to the press. As much as Katy Perry might have been straight as a ruler at heart, that didn't discourage Jessie from commenting on her "amazing boobs" and exchanging messages of admiration with her on Twitter. She also had a crush on Rihanna – after meeting her at the BRIT Awards, she claimed to be captivated by her "cute little nose" and labelled her a "hard-working hottie". Not only did Jessie say she wanted to be Rihanna, she also wanted to be with her. What was more, if rumours about the Barbadian's occasional lesbian flings were to be believed, she might have been in with a chance.

Yet the most direct come-on was yet to come. There was more romance in the air when then pink-haired rapper Nicki Minaj told MTV that she'd "fallen in love" with Jessie. She responded in return: "I love you too, Nicki... maybe it is a relationship that is waiting to be blossomed, can you imagine? What can you say when someone like Nicki Minaj says that they're in love with you? I am obsessed with her. I think that she's a superstar, she has taken that iconic thing to another level. To even have someone like her take time out of her busy schedule to know someone like me is just an honour... I think [she's] stupidly sick – I would be honoured if [she] wanted to work with me." Fuelling the rumours of a love match, Jessie added teasingly that she would "do anything" for her American counterpart.

Finally, when Jessie found herself plunged into a bizarre virtual love triangle between herself, glamorous actress Courteney Cox and her equally famous ex-husband David Arquette, she'd made it clear which gender her loyalties lay with.

The drama had started one afternoon in April when Jessie arrived at *Jimmy Kimmel Live!* with Kira a couple of paces behind, carrying her bags like the perfect female gentleman. Courteney too was on the US talk show that night, hoping to address some of the claims her ex had made about her following their bitter break-up. He'd taken to *The Howard Stern Show* to berate her and she'd had enough. "You can only take so much," she told the *Daily Mail*. "I would hear little snippets of what kind of person I am and I was like, 'You know what? I'm done!'"

She'd also heard that her ex-husband was infatuated with Jessie J – and, as she arrived on the show to defend her honour, was shocked to find herself about to come face to face with her love rival. "My publicist writes me and goes: 'You're not going to believe it – guess who's the musical guest?'" she'd recalled. Courteney had taken the news about Jessie being her ex's fantasy woman graciously, calling her "gorgeous" and confessing, "I don't blame him". However, she hadn't expected to be sharing the spotlight with her on the show — was it too close for comfort?

Jessie was there for very different reasons — her album had hit America on April 12 and she was desperate to show her face on national TV and remind the country of who she was. However, she was happy to make Courteney feel more comfortable when they shared a potentially awkward moment backstage. While Courteney told her she'd downloaded her album and enjoyed it, Jessie informed her: "If it means anything, I'd much rather date you than him!"

Aside from repeated sexuality scandals, the other time Jessie hit the news that month was when she outraged a group of young Irish people by appearing to condemn them as drunkards.

Jessie was already renowned for her teetotal lifestyle — she'd made that very clear in the media. "I don't drink. I don't smoke. I can't touch drugs. I can't even have caffeine. I have to be confident, because I can't intoxicate myself with these props ordinary young people have to give them confidence," she'd claimed.

Yet she'd then played at the Dublin Trinity Ball, something that the press had likened to an "orgy of music and drunkenness". Jessie was fine with the first part of the equation — she couldn't live without music. But as a young woman with a heart problem, she very literally couldn't live if she adopted a binge-drinking lifestyle. For that reason, she became increasingly uncomfortable when she played to a hall full of inebriated fans, some of whom were — apparently — barely conscious.

The moment she came off stage, she took to Twitter to rant: "Probably one of the hardest gigs to date. To see so many people so drunk they couldn't even stand. Girls unconscious and literally trampling on each other. It wasn't easy."

Ireland took it personally, and one gig-goer wrote back almost instantly, labelling her performance "shite". Desperate to explain, Jessie tried again: "I'm not upset they weren't all listening, it upset me to see so many young people not with it. Not used to it. It's hard to sing when I just wanted to go in the crowd and help all the crying girls being squashed."

Another angry fan retaliated: "Are you being serious? Just be thankful you were performing on stage to your fans." Jessie replied that she was "totally serious" and that it was "called caring about my fans". The following morning, she elaborated: "Can I just clear up that last night was a university ball and it was students. I was just shocked at how intoxicated they were and I was genuinely worried for them... It's not just in Ireland, it's everywhere. As a non-drinker, I just want to spread the message that binge drinking is dangerous. I just care."

Some took her comments as a snub against the Irish, until they discovered that Jessie herself was part Irish – just like her love idol Rihanna – and that she had family in County Clare.

Jessie had wanted to be an anti-drugs campaigner, but she was up against a tidal wave of rejection. One blogger asked incredulously: "Who is this Jessie J who questions how much we drink? Does she not understand that young Irish people love to party and get drunk to the point where they vomit down the front of their party outfits? What's your problem, Jessie?"

She was on a one-woman crusade against a world full of defiant drinkers, those who loved their lifestyles and had no intention of stopping. Could Jessie have just gained herself a reputation as the music world's biggest party-pooper? Had all her best intentions backfired?

The Mirror was the first newspaper to turn on her, claiming just two days after the show in Dublin that she lacked edge. "Jessie J claims she was shocked to see so many drunken fans," the paper wrote. "Now we know she doesn't drink or smoke and prides herself on being a good role model for fans. But did she really expect anything else at the Trinity Ball, which is known for its wild party atmosphere?" The review continued: "No one thinks it's a good idea to be so paralytic you can hardly stand. But can the scenes at the Trinity Ball have been so jawdroppingly dreadful? Jessie, we admire your clean-living lifestyle. But – whisper it now – it's hardly rock'n'roll, is it?"

Undoubtedly, Jessie couldn't compete in the rock'n'roll partying stakes. How could a girl with a heart complaint match the crack-smoking car-crash lifestyle of someone like Amy Winehouse? Amy had been earning headlines all over the world for what those who knew her described as her "inhuman", "unbelievable" limits in the drug department. She'd stretched her body to the max. She'd been a legend in life and had become a legend in death too, with some girls – many would say distastefully – gathering outside her front door to honour her life with a drunken party just days after her demise.

Whether it had been right or wrong, much of the world seemed to idolise fast living and hard partying, seeing it as the ultimate fantasy lifestyle. Jessie was the defiant antithesis of that path, insisting to *Time Out*: "Music is my drug and the only drug I'll ever want... I'm not someone who's anti, I just can't depend on it. Alcohol and drugs don't give me the confidence to be who I am and that's why I really wanna embrace being a role model. I want to show young people that you can be who you are with purity, you don't have to kind of infect it with a double shot of G&T or a spliff." She added: "Can you imagine me with alcohol? Not a good look... I'm irritating enough without it all."

She was attempting to take on the drinking habits of the millions with a weekend penchant for over-indulgence – did she really have a shot at changing them? Moreover, would they argue back that, like her song title, alcohol was part of who they were? Contrastingly, Jessie had wanted people to feel confident sober and in their own skin.

It wasn't looking good for Jessie on her mission, but it seemed that the message had been gratefully received by the *Irish Independent*, at least. The paper wrote: "Jessie J was hardly known outside of her bedroom 15 weeks ago... yet now she is an international phenomenon... [she] isn't just a singer, she's on a mission. She has a gospel and she's proselytising. She doesn't drink, smoke or do drugs and she preaches purity."

According to the reviewer, however, the message was an admirable one. She compared Jessie to The Black Eyed Peas music video 'I Gotta Feeling', which was described as "the most superb anthem to excess". "Its message is fill up your cup, let it overflow; if you go out at night, get smashed... in the last 60 seconds of this video, 10 girls fall down on the floor or in the street or in the gutter because they are drunk. The message from this music video to young women is you can't have a good time if you have enough brain cells to recall it the next day."

The paper continued: "Jessie J challenges all this... It's far too early to say if she will have any significant, lasting impact on global youth culture, but she is a very different role model from anything we've seen before."

Indeed, instead of creating a circus atmosphere around herself that had the paparazzi chasing in hot pursuit, Jessie was openly asking fans to "base your confidence on purity" – something the music world hadn't been associated with for a long time.

Jessie was also about to make another admission that was almost unknown for a female celebrity of her decade – with the song 'Nobody's Perfect', she reminded everyone of her flaws. The video was shot in the Bulgarian capital of Sofia and, like her other two singles, was directed by Emil Nava. This time, Jessie's world was transformed into a children's fairy-tale fantasy using scenery reminiscent of *Alice In Wonderland*. She sat at a banquet table that was inspired by the Mad Hatter's Tea Party name-checked in the story and she also sat atop a giant swing, experimental gothic make-up emblazoned across her face.

Jessie later appeared smothered in black paint, just like Rihanna had in her 'Rockstar' video, to depict a sinner, and then dressed all in white like a member of nineties R&B group TLC to portray a saint. Glow-in-the-dark neon eye make-up mimicked previous videos by Ke$ha and The Black Eyed Peas, but Jessie had put her own unique slant on the story. By the end, she sat alone as mice scurried across the deserted banquet table.

The track debuted on April 15 and became a Top 10 hit in the UK, Australia and New Zealand. "I'm so happy," Jessie told *The Sun*. "I think it's important to expose your flaws in music as well as your positives. As it says, nobody's perfect. I'm definitely not!"

The next step for Jessie was to plan her world tour. Fans were keen to know what to expect from her live – would she be sequinned and glamorous like Beyoncé, girly and sweet like Katy or downright outrageous like Gaga? Or perhaps she'd be keeping it simple like Amy Winehouse had done – just her and her backing singers, letting the music speak for itself.

Whatever she had in mind, it certainly wouldn't resemble Katy's tour. Jessie's biggest nightmare was the thought of wearing a pink frilly dress – according to her, the total antithesis of what her music stood for.

Yet she seemed confused about what she *would* offer. She'd told Clayton Perry: "People say to me: 'You're really raw. I can imagine your stage show to be like with you and a guitar.' And I'm like, 'No, that isn't it. I'm going to be like on top of a helicopter and have like fair dancers and like somersaults and shit... But like, I might do some forward rolls and some cartwheels... why not? There shouldn't be any limits or boundaries."

Meanwhile, Jessie seemed to contradict herself when she told *I Like Music*: "People always say: 'What can we expect? Will there be, like, a trapeze?' and I'm like: 'No! It'll be me, my band, an audience and good songs. That's all you need.' Perhaps by the second comment, her label had had a discussion with her about the budget.

Either way, her live shows were among the most hotly tipped of the year – until, on June 12, disaster struck. During rehearsals, Jessie collapsed in agony after one dance move too many injured her foot, forcing her to perform her show at the Capital Radio Summertime Ball on a gilded throne. There was worse news to come: what had at first seemed to be a suspected tendon injury was much more serious – she'd broken her foot in two places.

Undeterred, she still soldiered on through a challenging set at Glastonbury on June 25, when she invited a seven-year-old girl called Shae on stage to sing with her. Jessie had excitedly planned her grand entrance to one of the world's muddiest music festivals by joking that she'd don "wellies with six-inch heels". In reality, Jessie had her foot heavily bandaged and was confined to her throne again.

Days after a disappointing show, her management made an official statement, withdrawing her from a string of summer festivals: T in the Park, the iTunes festival, Lovebox and T4 on the Beach to name a few. After harrowing surgery on her foot, she needed time to "recuperate" before returning to the stage.

It wasn't the only foot-related mishap she'd suffered either. Back on June 2, she'd made a live debut on national TV show *Britain's Got Talent*. Dressed in a black leotard with a long sheer trail revealing what might have seemed the longest legs in pop and lip paint in the shades of the Union Jack flag, Jessie performed 'Mamma Knows Best'. Mischievously, she changed the words to "Simon knows best" in reference to the notoriously acid-tongued talent-show judge Simon Cowell.

However, halfway through her set, she suddenly stripped herself of her shoes. A puzzled *Daily Mail* journalist speculated: "Perhaps the height [of her heels] got the better of her." However, former dance tutor Dawn Wenn-Kober thought differently. "Her heel got caught in her dress," she told the author, "but she just slipped out of her shoes and carried on walking and didn't miss a note! People say, 'Oh, she's not wearing any shoes!' and I say, 'Well, she was at the beginning!'"

According to Dawn, it was her early training that had been the key to her reaction. "She copes so well and is just so professional to carry on performing like nothing's gone wrong – she was taught that from the beginning," Dawn explained. "Things will go wrong – but whatever happens, just keep going. If your costume falls to bits, you just carry on – that was something that was instilled in her right from the beginning until it came as second nature. She didn't get a chance to do it wrong when it was live theatre!"

Even barefoot, Jessie had been perfectly poised and serene, so she certainly wasn't going to let a little thing like a couple of broken bones destroy her shows. She made an incendiary return to the stage for the Big Chill festival in Hertfordshire on August 6, wearing a tight leopard-print all-in-one catsuit and a bright purple wig. She even wore a hat with pussycat ears suspended from it – and, despite yet again being confined to her throne, she was in good spirits.

She had to be – she had a schedule full of promotional events that she was determined not to miss. On August 4, she'd even joined Justin Timberlake and Mila Kunis on *Alan Carr: Chatty Man* by speeding in on a mobility scooter. Her sense of humour was as sharp as ever when the openly gay chat show host asked if she'd like a pouffe to rest her leg on, only to be met with the response: "I've already got one!"

Five days later, she had a heart-pounding moment in the studio when riots engulfed London, with buildings going up into flames. Looters were fleeing from shops with smashed-out windows, labouring under the weight of the plasma-screen TVs tucked under their arms, while screaming survivors flung themselves from their bedroom windows into the arms of rescuers. As the scene of carnage unfolded around her, the last thing Jessie wanted was to end up barricaded in the studio. What was more, with a broken foot, she could hardly run to safety. She'd been in the middle of writing a song when the building was abruptly evacuated but – rather than relying on her crutches – she had an aide on hand to carry her to safety.

Not to be defeated, Jessie simply wrote a song about the injustice of the riots when she returned. Fortunately, the destructive rampage hadn't disrupted her last-minute collaboration with dance DJ and producer David Guetta on the song 'Repeat'. When he heard from Jessie, he was so excited that he suspended the release of his album to guarantee she could be part of it. "The album was finished and then I got word from Jessie about this collaboration, so I called my label and said: 'Stop everything! The album can't go without this track!'" he recalled.

His album, *Nothing But The Beat*, released on August 29, might have had an impressive list of collaborators – Usher, Flo Rida, Timbaland, Ludacris, Akon, Snoop Dogg, will.i.am, Nicki Minaj and Lil Wayne – but, for David, it wasn't complete until Jessie had put her stamp on it too. In fact, it was such a last-minute operation that he was forced to produce the track from the lounge at Ibiza airport. "I would sit all day in the lounge with my headphones on, looking like a homeless person, finishing the vocal mix on my laptop!" he joked.

Jessie was also in demand with James Morrison, when the pair collaborated on a song called 'Up' for his album, *The Awakening*, which debuted on September 26. Both tracks saw her transcend the pain of a broken foot to get the recordings finished, and she was willing to grin and bear it at her video shoot for fourth single 'Who's Laughing Now' too. Perhaps she felt compelled to put on a brave face when journalists from *The Sun* gatecrashed the filming – nobody was going to see Jessie crack.

'Who's Laughing Now' was important to her as it showed off a range of influences. The lyrical content matched Christina Aguilera's 'Stronger' – both artists thanked their detractors for the pain they'd suffered at their hands, claiming it would make them tougher in the long run. Jessie also added a dose of her trademark humour, imitating the fairweather friends who'd cosied up to her after she found fame in a range of comedy voices. This part of the song emulated Lady Sovereign's '9 To 5', but it had an added helping of vocal acrobatics that the rapper had never attempted.

The song also dealt with a subject that Jessie knew from her Twitter messages was close to her fans' hearts: bullying. "[My bullies] now holler at me on Facebook saying, 'We should hang out'," Jessie recalled to *The Big Issue* of the track. "I'm like, 'Didn't you used to throw stones at me while I was walking home?' Just because I've become successful in what I do doesn't mean it rewrites the future – or the past."

Jessie had been keen to keep it real and focus on things that her fans could relate to in order to make her work meaningful to them, and 'Who's Laughing Now' had achieved that. "There's so many things that a 22-year-old girl can't relate to me with," she told Clayton Perry. "Being signed [is one of them] because I know that's so rare for a 22-year-old girl, so I feel like it's important for me to showcase the fact that I'm human too and that I go through normal stuff. I think it's so important that globally people relate to it."

The harrowing childhood Jessie had been through at the hands of haters was one many young people could understand, and Jessie recruited a preteen fan to play her younger self. Meanwhile she played several roles for her video part: a school teacher, a caretaker and a dinner lady. However, her injury meant she was confined to a wheelchair to get around the set. "The condition of doing the video is that I had to keep my foot raised," Jessie groaned. "I think it's great though and I wouldn't have it any other way."

The pain and inconvenience of the injury made her sympathetic to other sufferers and her charitable side came out when she decided to raise money for victims of similar injuries. "I have so much respect for people, young or old, who have ever had surgery on their bones," she tweeted. "We take walking, running, dancing for granted until we can't. I am so ready to get better and raise money for people who won't get better or won't walk again. Life is precious. Live it and love it."

That was her philosophy when she arrived at the V Festival in Chelmsford on August 20. She was carried on stage by a minder and propelled onto a giant lips-shaped sofa, one foot clad in a designer stiletto heel and the other bandaged in the obligatory cast. After one song, she discarded the heel on her healthy foot altogether and played the rest of the show barefoot. She teasingly dedicated 'Nobody's Perfect' to "anyone who's forgotten their sun cream" and brought a miniature version of herself on stage to play her childhood alter ago for the finale, 'Who's Laughing Now'.

Meanwhile Jessie also showed why she was a family girl when she changed the lyrics of 'Price Tag' to include sentiments like: "I just wanna make the Cornishes dance!" and told her family, who were waiting in the wings, how much she loved them. She rose to her feet for just a few minutes during 'Do It Like A Dude', but she fought off embarrassment to play the majority of the show seated and, despite the setbacks, her smile seemed to have been surgically attached to her face. "This is what happens when you break your foot – glamour goes out of the window!" she joked. "Roll with the punches, guys!"

The media was impressed by her sparkling demeanour. *Sugarscape* marvelled: "You've got to hand it to Jessie J – even with her broken foot, she put on a set better than the most acrobatic and nimble of us could have done!"

What was her trade secret? For those itching to know the magic formula, she'd been willing to share some of what she knew the following month when she'd appeared as a mentor on The *X Factor*. She might have hobbled in a little unsteadily on her crutches as she joined N-Dubz band member Tulisa Contostavlos in Mykonos to judge the groups category, but she was met with rapturous applause nonetheless.

While Jessie reported that all the new talent had made her feel insecure and anxious to step up her game, she needn't have worried – the MOBO Awards on October 13 proved she could still win over an audience. Jessie's appearance – even dressed down in Dr Martens and a drab baseball cap – was the talk of gossip columns across the country. She even overshadowed teenage songstress Dionne Bromfield, who'd given a show-stopping tribute to her late godmother Amy Winehouse when she'd covered 'Love Is A Losing Game'.

And that was just the start. After a spirited rendition of 'Do It Like A Dude' Jessie went on to win four of the five categories she'd been nominated for. Holding back the tears as she took to the stage to accept the trophy for Best Album, she gushed: "Wow, I did not expect to win that at all. I just want to say the biggest thank you to my fans because I watched this last year by myself in my living room and no one knew who I was and now I just won Best Album. This is epic!"

To prove just how fast her star had risen, her next award of the night was for Best Newcomer. From an unknown artist whose only claim to fame had been a few half-hearted listeners on YouTube to a widely renowned international icon, she'd come a long way – and all in less than a year. She went on to win the categories for Best Song ('Do It Like A Dude') and Best UK Act, losing out only on Best Video, which went to Tinchy Stryder and Dappy for 'Spaceship'.

However, not everyone welcomed Jessie's presence. As an annual awards ceremony dedicated to music of black origin, did her face and sound fit? According to black culture magazine *The Voice*, it didn't. Back in June, the publication had taken a swipe at white acts stealing the stage, arguing: "The MOBOs are doing a disservice to black artists by using white singers to push the show."

Not only did the controversial feature insist their presence was patronising to black talent, but it saw white faces as a mere marketing tool to seduce mainstream white audiences, marginalising ethnic singers in the process. The day after the ceremony, fellow singer Lily Allen – who by now had a reputation for celebrity spats, having made incendiary comments about Cheryl Cole and Katy Perry – unleashed her famous claws on Jessie via Twitter. "Now I love Jessie J as much as the next person," she claimed, "but how is her music of 'black origin'? Is it cause she says 'mandem' in her tune?"

However, songs like 'Stand Up' had hints of reggae, while several of her tracks were nods to Lauryn Hill and Whitney Houston – but perhaps the biggest validation of all for Jessie was the praise of the event's black founder, Kanya King. "Jessie's opening number?" she exclaimed. "I think people will remember that for a long time to come."

Already, Jessie had achieved the type of glowing praise many aspiring stars could only dream of – but she was far from finished. She was so keen to dedicate her life to music that she had a treble and bass clef encircled by a heart tattooed across her wrist. And if that wasn't enough to prove she was in it for the long haul, she'd spent her twenty-second birthday performing at a charity gig – a Teenage Cancer Trust night at London's Royal Albert Hall.

She'd aspired to be "an incredible genius like Beyoncé, with the longevity of Prince" but there was far more on Jessie's agenda than being a recording artist. She was desperate to pen her own musical and to open a string of charities, hospitals and homeless shelters around the country, too.

Elaborating on her plans, she told *I Like Music:* "I want to do campaigns, I want to dress up, I'd love to have my own TV show, I'd love to have my own clothing line, my own perfume... [and] I want to get a little friend for my BRIT. I'm hoping that's going to be a Grammy so they can hang out."

Aside from the glamour, Jessie was becoming quite a philanthropist for children, too. "I want to open youth centres across London to help kids out," she told PopDash. "My biggest dream in the whole world though is to open my own theme park... the rides would flow according to the different styles of my music. [The best ride] would be 'Do It Like A Dude', wouldn't it? I'd definitely want to go on that roller-coaster!"

She was dreaming big, but she also felt that even something as simple as a song could be a lifesaver. She'd already experienced that when a fan had written to her and confessed that hearing 'Who You Are' was the only thing that had stood between her and suicide. She hoped her legacy of "half-art, half-therapy" would continue.

Unlike people, songs were immortal and their messages often lived on. Jessie wanted to "heal the world" with hers. She'd broken away from her background and avoided the stereotypical fate of the Essex girls in her area – and while riots ripped through her hometown, she was on the festival circuit, celebrating her biggest shows of all time. She wanted to urge fans to live their dreams like she was doing, and not to let them go up in flames.

She was taking on a nation, if not a world, of binge drinkers and encouraging them to exercise self-restraint and celebrate purity. She was telling a nation of schoolgirls – who statistics showed would on average prefer to be a glamour model than a nurse – to dispense with the airbrushed images and the painted-on perfection, to stop agonising over imagined flaws and to simply be who they were. Those were Dr Jessie's orders.

Might she be the antithesis of the average pop star? What was more, in the pipeline was by far the biggest campaign of all. Pledging to save lives, she'd told Yin & Yang: "I discovered websites that give young people information on how to kill themselves quickly and painlessly, and it broke my heart. I've had bad health, so to me it's like, why would you abuse something that you've been given?"

She continued: "I wanted to start this online campaign, a place for people to go where they feel there's this little light in the world. I think that when you're 13 or 14, you might be questioning your sexuality or who you wanna be or how you wanna dress, or maybe you're being bullied or your mum and dad are fighting. I want there to be a place for [those people] where they know they're not alone... I will devote my life to saving other people because that's what I want music to be."

That was Jessie J's war cry – she was on a mission to make music that healed the world. What's more, those following her had a feeling that the journey had only just begun. She'd showed her bullies why she was truly worthy of 'Who's Laughing Now' as both a song title and a slogan – and now she just had to make the rest of the world laugh, too.

"I want to be at the top," she insisted. "You're not going to get rid of me."